Corporate Financial Advisers

Corporate Financial Advisers

Accelerators of company growth

LOUISE BROBY

 Prentice Hall
FINANCIAL TIMES

An imprint of Pearson Education

London ■ New York ■ Toronto ■ Sydney ■ Tokyo ■ Singapore ■ Hong Kong ■ Cape Town
New Delhi ■ Madrid ■ Paris ■ Amsterdam ■ Munich ■ Milan ■ Stockholm

PEARSON EDUCATION LIMITED

Head Office:
Edinburgh Gate
Harlow CM20 2JE
Tel: +44 (0)1279 623623
Fax: +44 (0)1279 431059

London Office:
128 Long Acre
London WC2E 9AN
Tel: +44 (0)20 7447 2000
Fax: +44 (0)20 7240 5771
Website: www.briefingzone.com

First published in Great Britain in 2002

© Pearson Education Limited 2002

The right of Louise Broby to be identified as author
of this work has been asserted by her in accordance
with the Copyright, Designs and Patents Act 1988.

ISBN 0 273 65641 4

British Library Cataloguing in Publication Data
A CIP catalogue record for this book can be obtained from the British Library.

10 9 8 7 6 5 4 3 2 1

Typeset by Monolith – www.monolith.uk.com
Printed and bound in Great Britain by Ashford Colour Press Ltd, Gosport, Hants.

The Publishers' policy is to use paper manufactured from sustainable forests.

About the author

Louise Broby is a financial writer who has written extensively on a wide range of topics. Her publications include *Investment Regulation in Europe*, *Global Stock Markets*, *Pan-European Financial Regulation* and *Stock Market Globalisation*. She has worked in investment banking and as a business school academic. Louise may be contacted at:

Stratos Multimedia
6th Floor
175 Piccadilly
London W17 9TB

Tel: 07802 882 554
Fax: 020 7449 7517
Email: lb@stratos.demon.co.uk

Contents

Tables

Figures

Preface

The appalling terrorist attacks on the New York World Trade Centre twin towers on Tuesday 11 September 2001 and the momentous and tragic loss of innocent human lives were an unspeakable violation of the freedom of the US and the world. Above all, these events constituted a direct attack not only on the symbol of the US financial system but also on the entire infrastructure of the capitalist system itself. Seriously wounded, US markets momentarily ceased to function. The New York Stock Exchange and Nasdaq closed, for the first time in history, for four consecutive days.

But the financial world immediately began to fight back, baring the human face of finance in an extraordinary display of support and courage. The financial industry leaders expressed their deep shock and sadness at the loss of life, and courageously rallied in showing unrivalled solidarity and defiance. The industry came together in an expression of grief and condemnation, and although seriously impaired, showed its will to fight back and to rebuild the fractured links in the financial system. Rallying around their financial services clients were the IT suppliers who immediately formed an alliance to help their clients restore their trading and other operations.

Many of the financial services firms had already prepared for the eventuality of terrorist attack and had backed up and stored their data in remote locations. Morgan Stanley and Deutsche Bank announced that they had successfully transferred client data to back-up support facilities.

The major US and global financial institutions posted messages of condolences and sympathy on their websites. Declarations ranged from promising to restore the financial system to rebuilding the nation's confidence.

In the week following the attack, full-page advertisements appeared in British newspapers to pay tribute to those lost.

Excerpts of messages posted on the internet included:

- **Merrill Lynch**

  Merrill Lynch immediately set up a 'command headquarters' in Lower Manhattan when their headquarters in the World Financial Centre across the street from the collapsed towers was closed. Their website contained this message: 'We extend our thoughts and prayers to the thousands of people affected. We mourn the loss of our colleagues and friends, and grieve for their families. We will also never forget the courage of the police, fire and rescue personnel who risked their lives, and in some cases gave their lives, to help others ... History has shown the resilience of our financial system in times of crisis. We are confident that, as in the past the global financial markets will prevail and go forward with renewed strength. In the face of great tragedy, freedom-loving people throughout the world will join Americans to move forward with compassion, courage and strength.'

- **Goldman Sachs**

'We are all saddened by the horrific destruction and loss of life resulting from the terrorist attacks in the United States on 11 September. Our thoughts and prayers are with those many people and organizations who are suffering from this terrible tragedy.

'At Goldman Sachs, we share the strong determination of the entire securities industry to show solidarity in the face of terrorism. We are sending the clearest possible message that terrorists will not close free markets.'

- **Morgan Stanley**

'We are all saddened and outraged by the attack on America today, and extend our deepest sympathies and prayers to all the people affected.

'While our key focus and concern are for the well-being and safety of our colleagues, and families who worked in the WTC, we want our clients and regulators to know that in spite of this tragedy, all of our businesses are functioning and will continue to function.

'All our clients should rest assured that their assets are safe. We are committed to resuming full operation as exchanges and markets re-open.'

- **J.P. Morgan Chase & Co**

A message from Bill Harrison, President and CEO: 'We remain shocked, saddened and outraged by Tuesday's terrorist attack. In the immediate hours after the attack, our leadership team identified two priorities, supporting colleagues directly impacted by the tragedy and implementing our contingency plans designed to maintain client service and continuity.'

- **Lehman Brothers**

Chairman and CEO Richard S. Fuld, jr:

'The tragic attack on the World Trade Centre and the resulting damage have shocked and saddened us all. Our thoughts go out to the victims and their families. Our first priority is to make sure that we are doing everything possible for the health and safety of our employees.'

- **UBS**

'UBS remains profoundly shocked by the attacks in the US and by the scale of personal tragedy. UBS's deepest sympathies lie with those who have loved ones, relatives, friends or colleagues among the victims.'

- **Bear Stearn**

Following the attack, Bear Stearn called a meeting of industry leaders to show support and solidarity. At the meeting, several industry leaders offered tangible help in the form of office space for impaired colleagues with computer access and software if needed. Bear Stearn posted the following internet message:

'Bear Stearn is saddened and outraged by the tragic losses from the attacks on America. Our hearts and prayers go out to our colleagues, friends and families and all those who have suffered as a result of this most terrible act. Bear Stearn is committed to being part of the effort to rebuild the nation's confidence.'

- **Barclays Capital**

'We are shocked and saddened by the events in New York City, Washington DC and Pittsburgh on Tuesday 11 September. Our deepest sympathies are with the families and friends of those affected by this tragedy.

In spite of the temporary loss of our primary New York office, all on Barclay's businesses are working diligently to ensure minimal disruption to all our businesses in North America.'

- **Barclays Bank** in the UK joined in supporting their colleagues:

'Following the tragic events in America, we will do everything that we can to help those customers who have been directly affected by the situation. We are deeply saddened by the attack on America and we extend our deepest sympathies to all the people affected.

'Our customer services teams will handle all requests for assistance with the utmost sympathy and we will do all that we can to provide access to funds to customers caught up in these tragic events.'

- **PricewaterhouseCoopers**

'Connecting with each other in a moment of overwhelming loss: As members of the global community, PricewaterhouseCoopers extends its heartfelt condolences to the families and friends of all those who perished in this shocking disaster – in the aeroplanes, the World Trade Centre and the Pentagon. We mourn along with you for our lost PricewaterhouseCoopers' colleagues, clients, associates, friends and family. Our resolve is to provide support and assistance in every way we can.'

- **Andersen**

Andersen, accountants and consultants, also expressed their condolences:

'The 85 000 professionals of Andersen around the world send their sympathies and thoughts to those hurt in the recent acts of terrorism, and hopes and best wishes to the many rescue workers and volunteers helping to rebuild.'

- **Instinet (a Reuters company)**

Instinet sent out this message from Doug Atkin, President and CEO:

'Yesterday's terrorism puts into perspective for each of what is truly important in life, what we each truly work for – the well-being and safety to those closest to us – our families and friends, and for Instinet that also means our employees and colleagues around the world.

'Despite this tragedy, the US financial markets will be up and running again soon, and we are in touch with industry and government officials regarding the steps that we can take.'

- **HSBC**

The CEO of HSBC, Keith Whitson, said:

'We are deeply shocked by the tragic events, which took place in the United States on 11 September. On behalf of everyone at HSBC, I would like to extend our heartfelt sympathy to colleagues, to the families and friends of the bereaved and injured and to all the American people at this distressing time.'

- **American Express** located in the opposite World Trade Financial Centre, said on their website:

'The multiple attacks carried out against the US on 11 September represent one of the greatest tragedies of modern times. Our thoughts and prayers go out to everyone who was affected by these devastating events.

'The attacks on the World Trade Centre in New York had an immediate impact on the US financial system, and on the American Express headquarters building, which is located in the World Financial Centre in Lower Manhattan. Despite this tragedy, all of our businesses around the world are operating and will continue to function. Whilst our company's corporate headquarters is currently inaccessible, our client service centres are located around the world. We maintain electronic records of our records at several locations across the US and around the world. Data and records pertaining to your accounts with us are safe.'

- **Nasdaq**

The CEO of Nasdaq, Hardwick Simmons, offered condolences and issued a defiant statement.

'Friends:

We at Nasdaq want to offer our deepest condolences and prayers to the families of the many everyday heroes who are the victims of this tragedy. We want to assure you that the Nasdaq market will be open in the coming days. We are testing our systems and those of our members as I write. This is important and significant. A sign that our great nation will not be intimidated. We will conduct our affairs in the same way that we always do. Nasdaq and the American capital markets are about freedom and opportunity for all. We will continue in our mission to enable a stronger, more robust world for all of our citizens. The American capital markets are sound. Nasdaq will be open.'

- **The SEC** whose enforcement office was destroyed, lost hundreds of files and computer records on sensitive investigations, including insider trading. They took immediate action to facilitate the re-opening of markets, describing them as 'the world's strongest and most vibrant, in spite of the heinous acts of last Tuesday.'

  For the first time ever, emergency powers were invoked to ease certain regulatory restrictions, and additional market information was posted on its website.

- **The Bank of England and the Financial Services Authority** issued a joint declaration of sympathy and support on their website:

  'The UK financial markets are operating in an orderly fashion, albeit in highly abnormal circumstances, following the tragic events in the US.

  'The UK markets have been monitoring developments very closely both here and overseas. We have been in close touch with the US and other overseas authorities and will work together to seek to resolve any problems that may arise from these events.'

Executive summary

OVERVIEW

The business world is changing rapidly, and the race for supremacy in the corporate environment is gathering momentum. To survive and stay ahead of competitors, corporations need the best possible advice from their financial advisers. The changing marketplace in turn places new demands on the advisers who are forced to move from local scenarios to global arenas and advance their expertise and pool of knowledge to enable them to meet the new challenges and service their clients effectively.

Through the use of this Executive Briefing, decision-takers in multinationals or large corporations and small and medium-sized enterprises (SMEs) will be able to form a good idea of how to select and utilize their corporate financial advisers. With the advent of the global economy, which affects all businesses, large or small, the contribution the financial advisers can make, is rapidly changing and expanding. Within this new scenario, executives need to know the criteria for seeking the right financial advisers. With changing circumstances, how can the financial advisers' contribution be applied to maximum corporate advantage?

The FT Executive Briefing in its Introduction emphasizes the overall role of financial advisers as accelerators of growth. It is their behind-the-scenes work that enables companies to target the right finance sources for expansion. They steer the companies through the myriad of formalities required for mergers and acquisitions (M&As) or for listings or multiple listings on the stock market, and they advise on the optimal organization structure for any given strategy.

A profile of the corporate financial advisers is presented, together with the companies they serve. Their main areas of expertise are specified. The increasing globalization of stock markets has implications for their work in terms of additional sectoral expertise. The financial advisers have to adapt to a climate of change involving economic downturns and vacillations in sectors such as e-commerce, not to mention the impact of terrorism on investor confidence around the world.

CHAPTER CONTENT

- Chapter 1 examines the factors impacting on the selection of corporate financial advisers. Making the right choice of advisers is crucial for commercial success. Factors to look for include the level of expertise of the financial advisers, and special sector-based expertise, which may be needed in certain industries such as biotechnology and the IT sector. Through their dealings, the financial advisers will have gained a reputation, perhaps in specific areas, and in some cases, financial advisers are selected on the basis of reputation alone.

- It is also important for the client to ensure that there is synergy between the financial advisers' *modus operandi* and company strategies. Are the financial advisers of a size commensurate with the size of the deal envisaged, and do they have the right access to capital markets? Also important is the question of fees.

- Chapter 2 focuses on the top league of financial advisers and their teams, which comprise other professional advisers such as accountants, lawyers and PR specialists. Where available, rankings and comparisons of financial advisers on a number of criteria are included, such as their market capitalization or type of client. The top league of financial advisers in terms of M&A deal value is also presented.

- The United States plays a dominant role in the world economy, and the largest international financial advisers are US-based, with offices all over the globe. This is the theme of Chapter 3. The corporate financial advisers in the United States lead the world in terms of turnover, number of clients and size of deals. Some of the top financial advisers, such as Morgan Stanley, Merrill Lynch, Goldman Sachs and Lehman Brothers are singled out in terms of the nature of their work, their performance and their global reach.

- In Chapter 4, the financial advisers' main fund-raising activities and sources of finance are discussed. Funding activities range from early-stage financing through to public offerings. Financial advisers can contribute to the financial strategies of corporations on a national or international scale. Their role spans from the early years of a company's existence when the company may need advice on day-to-day activities, financial planning and capital raising, through to the fully developed up-and-running company which in addition to on-going financial advice may need direction on its strategic plans for development and expansion.

- Chapter 5 focuses on one of the main areas of activity of the financial advisers, i.e., bringing companies to the stock market through a flotation. Competent financial advisers will make sure their client company does not go forward to a listing before it has met all the relevant criteria, and they will guide the company through the flotation itself. In the follow-up phase, after the initial public offering (IPO) on a recognized stock exchange, the role of the financial advisers has not ended. They will ensure that the company keeps in touch with investors and remains in the public eye, through constant monitoring, research and analysis. The reasons for listing are discussed, and the phases in the flotation process are explained. The chapter includes a checklist of the tasks to be carried out and the procedures to be followed by the IPO candidates. The UK's two main markets, the London Stock Exchange and AIM, are described.

- Much of the work of the financial advisers in connection with organizing a flotation for a company involves the preparation of documents, the focus of Chapter 6. Preceding the flotation, a business plan will have been prepared. The business plan, drawn up by the company itself, with or without an input from the financial advisers, will play an important part in formulating subsequent flotation strategies, and a checklist of such a plan is included. An essential document for a flotation is the prospectus, which is prepared by the financial advisers together with the company.

- Chapter 7. Another major area of activity for the financial advisers is mergers and acquisitions (M&A). Through the M&A process, companies expand into or withdraw from markets either in their home country or internationally. The role of the financial adviser is not only to obtain the best deal for their clients. They take a wider approach, starting with identification and valuation of the appropriate target, and after the deal is consummated, they offer further advice on how to merge or integrate the entities involved. The financial advisers aim to help clients maximize returns from their M&A activity, whether it be acquisitions, alliances, mergers or divestitures. The deal process is explained, together with the information required for the M&A process. The work of the Takeover Panel is discussed. To elucidate the size of deals, tables showing recent M&A activity are included.

- Chapter 8 sets out regulatory issues impinging on the financial advisers and their work. The roles of the Bank of England and the FSA in regulating the financial sector are outlined. The framework of EU financial services directives is set out, with reference to major individual directives. New directives relating to electronic financial services are also referred to.

- Case study. A case study of the well-established UK financial advisers Close Brothers, is presented in Chapter 9. The company's business model and structural approach are outlined. Internationally, the company has developed a unique organizational strategy based on takeovers and alliances in key markets, including European, Asian markets and the US.

- Chapter 10 contains a summary of conclusions of the FT Executive Briefing, together with an overall conclusion.

Acknowledgements

The author is grateful for the invaluable advice and guidance given by the Financial Times Prentice Hall Executive Briefings Senior Acquisitions Editor, Laurie Donaldson, and should also like to thank the many corporate financial advisers who have given enthusiastic support and provided research material for the book.

Introduction

ACCELERATORS OF GROWTH

Corporate financial advisers act as accelerators of company growth. This role is not always appreciated to the full by the companies that benefit. In many cases, the financial advisers are the unsung heroes of a company's success. Apart from the financial press, news media in general hardly give a mention to the financial advisers behind successful fundraisings or deals. Yet it is through the specialist contribution of the financial advisers that companies are able to raise large sums of finance in the markets. The advisers shape the fate of the companies for years to come through arranging mergers and acquisitions, initial public offerings on recognized stock exchanges (IPOs), de-mergers, spin-offs and other transactions. They act as dynamos in driving companies forward to take their place in local and global markets, and it is only through their superior expertise in dealing with financial issues that the companies end up raising millions of pounds.

The advisers are the ones responsible for promoting company shares before and after a flotation, and for creating value by constantly ensuring that the companies retain high visibility after being brought to market, thus maintaining investors' interest. Equally, if a company wants to raise finance for expansion, the financial adviser will advise on the best way of doing this, whether it is via the stock market or via banking sources. A company may want to rationalize its organization structure, and the financial advisers will guide the company through to an optimal solution.

CREATORS OF INDIVIDUAL WEALTH

Also not to be overlooked is the role the corporate financial advisers play in arranging for investors, promoters, principals, company executives and other employees to benefit from their deals through the creation of individual wealth. Exit strategies formulated by the financial advisers allow venture capitalists a profitable exit route, whereby they will recoup their investment at considerably greater percentage rates of return than would be possible on straightforward lending of money.

Promoters and key individuals receive shares or are allowed to convert their share options. If the options are exercised, they can make the option holders into instant millionaires. Employee share option schemes reward employees who stay on in a company following flotation or takeovers, and also attract the top executives needed for top-drawer flotations. Many of the high-net-worth individuals (HNWIs) and ultra-high-net-worth individuals in the United States owe their newfound riches to IPOs of dot.com and other companies orchestrated by the corporate financial advisers.

The financial advisers have a vested interest in making money for their clients since they also make substantial gains for themselves. They ensure an early exit route for any initial finance they may have arranged, as well as a maximum return on any share option they may hold. Equity stakes, especially in the US are not uncommon.

The financial advisers also assist companies in achieving performance targets through effective use of their high-level contacts for the purpose of recruiting board members who will benefit their clients in business terms. They may for instance, recommend the appointment of a retired general to the board of a client defence company, with the unspoken aim of gaining lucrative defence contracts for their client.

A PROFILE OF CORPORATE FINANCIAL ADVISERS

Entities acting as corporate financial advisers include securities firms, broker/dealers, investment management firms, commercial banks, merchant banks and investment banks. In a support role to the financial advisers are a host of professional advisers, including law firms, accountants/auditors, taxation experts, real-estate advisers, insurance companies, intellectual-property advisers, public relations (PR) firms, investor relations consultants and others.

Corporate financial advisers have as their clients the full range of companies from start-ups through SMEs (small and medium-sized enterprises) to major listed companies, both domestic and international. International companies may have a presence in one or two other countries, or be represented right round the globe.

Financial advisers representing global companies tend to be global themselves, with offices in major financial centres.

Finance has only recently been recognized as a separate academic discipline, with some universities running courses on investment, evaluation techniques, portfolio management and other related topics. Membership of various professional institutes also bestows recognition.

The City University in London offers a BSc in investment, finance and risk, covering subjects such as investment and financial risk management, risk analysis and insurance, with electives such as financial services regulation and forex markets.

Stirling University in Scotland offers a finance degree programme with courses on, *inter alia*, corporate finance decisions, securities and investment, international finance, and financial analysis.

The FPC (financial planning certificate) is an established qualification for financial advisers. It is recognized by various regulators and leads to membership of the Society of Financial Advisers. Their courses give a good grounding in financial products and knowledge of regulatory requirements under the Financial Services Act. An Advanced Finance Planning Certificate is also available.

Accountants, who also offer services in the financial services field, have long had their own qualifications. The ACA qualification can be obtained through the Institute of Chartered Accountants in England and Wales, or the Institute of Chartered Accountants in Scotland. The ACCA (the Association of Chartered Certified Accountants) is a worldwide body, and offers the ACCA qualification. This qualification is linked to the requirements of the modern business world. Other accountancy associations include the Chartered Institute of Management Accountants, the Chartered Institute of Public Finance and Accountancy. Accountancy-related qualifications which are useful to financial advisers, can be obtained in taxation, actuarial studies, information systems auditing and financial planning.

Corporate financial advisers give advice in a number of areas. Broadly, advice is given on short-term and long-term corporate financial strategy, including future strategies. They make recommendations on the best strategies for corporate expansion, and if necessary contraction. Corporate growth is every with-profit organization's chosen path; but if economic circumstances dictate, contraction may be necessary for survival in the longer term. In a recession, with orders drying up, companies may have no choice but to shed unprofitable subsidiaries. The financial advisers will assist in minimizing the financial damage of such an exercise, or even in raising cash through selling off unprofitable units. With technological advance, products may become outdated and unsaleable, requiring a shift in the direction of the company, and a re-assessment of priorities. The financial advisers will help with restructuring and market analysis, which will help companies identify marketing strategies to target opportunities effectively.

The financial advisers' expertise in developing long-term capital structures to match the companies' future strategies saves painful changes later. Creating the right capital structures will benefit client firms and their investors in the long run. Experienced advisers will ensure that the structuring is expedient and viable not only for immediate requirements, but for future eventualities such as rights issues, takeovers, dividends and share options.

The handling of and advice on mergers and acquisitions is one of the main areas of expertise of the financial advisers. They manage the entire process from looking for suitable acquisitions for growth, identifying targets, buyers and sellers, or partners for mergers and alliances, to negotiating the deal, and implementation of the takeover or merger. Due to the volume of deals they are involved in, they end up as experienced negotiators and will extract the best possible deal for their clients.

For a while, M&A markets were booming, and many financial advisers began to turn to international deals of the order of £1 billion rather than smaller domestic ones. But with the recent stagnation in the markets, the big deals are becoming a rare occurrence.

Financial advisers also specialize in raising funds through IPOs (flotations), private equity, private placements, banking finance or other sources of funding. Once a company is up and running, the advisers will assist in raising further finance, for instance through seeking additional private or institutional sources.

THE IMPACT OF GLOBALIZATION

In recent years, the demand for advice from financial advisers on a global scale has expanded enormously. As companies are internationalizing, so they are changing their narrow strategic thinking with restricted vision into a cross-border approach with financial advice and services extending into hitherto untapped new areas. Financial advisers are meeting this new challenge by similarly expanding globally and adding to the range and scope of services they are offering. The most successful financial organizations embracing this new playing field are becoming larger and operating on a global scale, with smaller more specialized firms being the target of takeovers from the bigger firms wanting their focused expertise as part of a broad spectrum of facilities they can offer mutinationally.

In the global arena, financial advisers handle issues that are specific to international companies. Choosing the right domicile in terms of tax regimes becomes important, as do matters such as restrictions on the movement of capital in and out of countries, the right to expatriation of profits, tax incentives, currency risks, political stability, etc. On such matters, the financial advisers will call in experts, either from their own company or from outside.

Financial advisers are increasingly involved in cross-border mergers and takeovers. Since the setting up of the EU single market, cross-border alliances and M&As have become much more attractive, and cross-border alliances are on the increase. Globally, transatlantic deals have increased, with much of the investment going from Europe to the United States.

The financial advisers themselves are expanding globally, but with recession looming, and M&A activity declining, the rate of expansion is slowing down, and unprofitable operations are coming under scrutiny.

With the increasing globalization of stock markets, companies are becoming more aware of the opportunities for tapping into international sources of funds. One way of doing this is to seek dual or multiple listings on exchanges around the world. This requires extra expertise on the part of the financial advisers who have to prepare companies in local markets for international flotation, with all that this involves in terms of international accounting standards, due diligence processes and legal, regulatory and taxation differences in the various countries.

A CLIMATE OF CHANGE

For a couple of years, financial advisers and their high-tech clients were riding high on a wave of dot.com euphoria, but this era has come to an end. Technology, however, is here to stay. Not all the dot.com companies are collapsing. Many of the early ventures that managed to consolidate and expand before everyone jumped on the bandwagon, are surviving, despite ups and downs, restructurings and layoffs. And some are making profits. With technology coming of age, IT still has enormous potential. Much expertise has been gained in the evaluation of high-tech companies; and this is likely to stand the industry in good stead in future flotations, which are not likely to reach the ballooning evaluations of the dot.com golden age. Investors, scared off by the huge swings in tech stocks, have turned to brick-and-mortar-related opportunities, and corporate financial advisers have picked up on their traditional role of providing advice and seeking funding for such companies. Old economy businesses are seeing a revival of interest from investors looking for safe havens, but the recent terrorist attacks on the World Trade Centre have seen yet another shift in investors' preferences, and defensive stocks and bonds have come to the fore.

Another aspect of change is the growing advisory involvement of the big accountancy firms, with up to 10 per cent of income coming from corporate finance and related work in the taxation, audit and legal fields. The big firms have established an international presence over many years, and are well positioned to serve international clients.

PLANNING FOR THE FUTURE

Financial advisers have an essential part to play in planning future strategies for companies, whether the companies are existing entities or newly formed entities through M&As. An important component in an M&A is the exit strategy for those involved. A successful exit strategy is important for company owners, shareholders and other interested parties. A reliable team of M&A experts is required to develop such a strategy.

Factors affecting the selection of corporate financial advisers

OVERVIEW

Financial success is at the very heart of for-profit commercial organizations, and with the globalization of business, the contribution of financial advisers has become one of the most essential ingredients for corporate survival, development and growth.

In recent years, the demand for advice from financial advisers on a global scale has expanded enormously. As companies are internationalizing, so they are changing their narrow strategic thinking and restricted vision into a cross-border approach with financial advice and services extending into hitherto untapped new areas. Financial advisers are meeting this new challenge by similarly expanding globally and adding to the range and scope of services they are offering. The most successful financial organizations embracing this new playing field are becoming larger and operating on a global scale. They are on the look-out for smaller more specialized firms as targets for takeovers. The focused expertise of the smaller firms is a useful addition to the broad spectrum of facilities offered by the larger firms in local and international markets.

MAKING THE RIGHT CHOICE

In this environment, the importance of choosing the right corporate financial advisers cannot be over-estimated. The implementation of their recommendations on how to plan present and future business strategies can pay dividends many times over, and can make the difference between success and failure in the fiercely competitive corporate environment. Reputable financial advisers lend strength to any corporation large or small. The backing of a top firm of financial advisers sets the corporation apart from competitors and paves the way for capital-raising and other transactions in an increasingly complex financial regulatory framework.

The appointment of financial advisers is a board-level decision, yet many board members and senior directors, due to an overload of commitments, find it difficult to keep up with the changing nature of financial advice in a rapidly globalizing world. This niche focus report fills a vital gap in the existing knowledge-base available to high-level decision-takers, and it is an invaluable tool for them to keep abreast of the latest strategic thinking in gaining a competitive advantage through the use of the right financial advisers.

EXPERTISE

To judge the expertise of the financial advisers it is not enough to read their promotional literature since this tends to be very general, and to span the entire range of advisory activities, from fund-raising transactional expertise, origination of M&A deals, management buy-outs (MBOs), management buy-ins (MBIs), disposals, IPOs, etc. The advisers should be recognized by a national professional body, such as the FSA. As an independent body and regulator of the financial services industry, the FSA has statutory powers under the Financial Services Act 1983 and the Banking Act 1987. They maintain a central register of financial firms, which can be used for checking out whether a particular financial services firm is authorized to carry out investment within the UK. One of the objectives of the FSA is to protect investors. They also offer protection to firms utilizing the services of its recognized advisers, in case anything goes wrong with the investment firm. Established financial advisers are also Nominated Financial Advisers to quoted companies on the London Stock Exchange.

Sector-based expertise

A company seeking to raise funds in the primary market may also have to consider whether it needs a financial adviser with special expertise in a particular sector, such as biotechnology or healthcare. A company such as Beeson Gregory, for instance, has a strong expertise in high-tech companies. The company has brought some 40 technology companies to technology-orientated exchanges and new markets (Nasdaq, TechMARK, AIM).

It is also an advantage if the financial advisers know the market for a company's products, since they will then be better able to assess the company's potential in terms of future orders and relevance of product type or technology. Are there any products or product developments which are new to the market, and which therefore provide the 'sizzle' of an offering?

REPUTATION IN THE MARKETPLACE

The reputation of the financial adviser is built up over many years, and is often assessed through word of mouth. The financial advisers themselves will often help the client along by pointing out that they have a reputation for efficiency in a particular area, such as closing deals, etc. This sort of promotion is of course likely to be biased. A good way of assessing the pedigree of a company is to look at past deals. Who are their clients? Are they of any substance? The financial advisers will usually supply a list of corporate clients, if asked. Various professional publications, such as *Euromoney*, run competitions, and give awards for excellence in the marketplace. League tables such as those published by Hemscott and Thomson Financial also give indirect guidance as to the standing of the financial firms.

The integrity of corporate financial advisers is paramount, and where this falls down, or is called into question, such as in the case of Andersen's auditing of Enron's accounts, it has severe repercussions – not only for the financial advisers themselves, but for the financial community as a whole.

SYNERGY WITH THE CLIENT COMPANY'S FINANCIAL STRATEGIES

The client company may have definite strategies about their future plans, or they may call in the financial advisers to help them formulate and implement such strategies. If for instance, the company has identified a weakness in its financial planning process, and it needs help in evaluating its investment and financing strategies, financial advisers can point the company in the right direction. The client may want the adviser to re-examine its long-term strategic planning, and to define how this can best be achieved. The client might also benefit from an independent assessment of its growth potential within the constraints imposed by internal and external factors. For firms with complicated tax and accounting issues, a firm of accountants as advisers may be the answer.

If on the other hand, a firm has decided to expand through the pursuit of an M&A strategy, it will be well-served by calling in a high-profile investment firm which specializes in deal-making, such as Goldman Sachs, Merrill Lynch and Morgan Stanley.

For IPOs, candidates again have to consider the reputation of the financial advisers. The name of a strong financial adviser on the front page of the IPO prospectus can sell an issue before anyone has even read the contents. It is up to the companies to prove that they can justify becoming accepted as an IPO candidate in terms of future profitability, financial standing, viability, market potential, etc.

RELATIVE SIZE OF THE CLIENT COMPANY AND ITS FINANCIAL ADVISERS

Only large companies can afford the fees of the big names in corporate finance. However, small and mid-sized companies are increasingly in need of competent financial advisers as they reach out for European and global markets. At the same time, many of the financial advisers are increasingly turning their attention to the small and medium-sized market, one reason being that there are only a limited number of really big deals to go around.

M&A DEAL SIZE

Whatever the size of an M&A deal, the corporate financial advisers selected should show a track record of successful deals of a similar size. If the deal runs into millions or billions, a large firm of corporate financial advisers is recommended, since they are more likely to be structured to encompass the breath of expertise needed in such a deal. They will also have the experience necessary to structure a complex deal in financial terms, as well as raising the necessary funds on behalf of their client.

With a decline in the number of M&As, some financial advisers may be prepared to go for lesser deals than they would otherwise have been prepared to undertake. Major companies such as UBS Warburg target deals for companies with a market capitalization of between £100 million and £1 billion. Andersen reports that deals they will handle, can be up to £1 billion or above in size. The maximum size in deals handled by Andersen has grown from around £500 million a couple of years ago. KPMG tends to go for deals of less than £1 billion. At Close Brothers, a typical deal size is £500 million, but the company also looks at the future prospects of potential clients, with an eye to establishing a longer-term relationship.

CLIENT LIST/RECOMMENDATIONS

Many financial advisers publish their client list on their website or in other literature. Lists of companies and deal sizes are also published by research organizations. An examination of such lists will give an idea of the type of clients the financial advisers typically serve. The financial advisers may also post client testimonials on their site or print them in their promotional literature. Word of mouth recommendations by business colleagues or referrals also instil confidence in the choice of corporate financial advisers.

INTERNATIONAL PRESENCE

If a company wants to take over a company with its main base in another country, say, Hong Kong, the financial adviser appointed should preferably have an office or some form of representation in that location, for instance through an alliance with a local firm.

For companies wanting to seek a listing on a stock market in a country other than their home country, such as a UK firm going for a Nasdaq listing, it is preferable to have US financial advisers, or UK financial advisers with a presence in the United States. The US advisers will be *au fait* with the regulatory regime in the US and will be familiar with the most effective way of obtaining approval for a listing.

LEAD MANAGERS/CO-MANAGERS

For a large issue, a lead manager and possibly co-managers have to be appointed. The role of the lead manager is to act as the leader of an underwriting syndicate, and it is regarded by the financial advisers as being the prime position, especially since underwriting fees are highly lucrative. The lead manager manages the transaction and is normally responsible for contact with the borrower, for the structure, organization and text of the loan agreement and prospectus, as well as for the composition of the underwriting syndicate and the selling group and, ultimately, for the placement itself.

The choice of a lead manager can make or break an issue. If the lead manager is one of the big firms, the issue will practically sell itself. Whilst a smaller firm has to go cap in hand to persuade a top company to take on the role of lead manager, in major issues, such as privatization programmes, the major investment banks will compete in bidding for the role as lead manager. In the privatization of the Port of Singapore Authority, for instance, six companies (Credit Suisse First Boston, Goldman Sachs, Morgan Stanley, Nomura, Salomon Smith Barney and UBS Warburg) all presented competing bids for the role.

However, smaller mid-market firms with capital requirements between US$ 5 million and US$ 40 million may benefit from having a smaller investment bank as common stock lead manager or co-manager, since the smaller firm may not receive adequate attention from the larger investment bank, whereas a smaller co-manager may provide a more aggressive timely approach, and may also provide better after-market support, such as market-making and research coverage.

Co-managers to the issue also help to sell the issue, although sometimes, they do very little work. The lead manager benefits from having a hardworking co-manager to support his efforts. However, too many co-managers on an offering may complicate the process of selling the issue, since co-ordination becomes more difficult. Co-managers specializing in a particular sector are of value since the institutional buyers may wish a more in-depth insight into an issue and its place within a particular industry sector which the buyers may not be able to obtain from the management of the company of the issue itself.

In M&As, the financial advisers act as lead advisers. Lead advisers in recent £100 million plus takeovers were PricewaterhouseCoopers (Britax/Seton), JP Morgan (Ascot PLC/Dow UK) and Deutsche Bank (PT Plc, Bromley Property Investments Ltd). In large billion-pound takeovers, there tend to be several advisers: e.g. Billiton Plc/BHP Ltd had UBS Warburg, JP Morgan, Gresham Advisory and Dresdner Kleinwort Wasserstein, and Blue Circle/Lafarge SA had Dresdner Kleinwort Wasserstein and Schroder Salomon Smith Barney.

CONFLICT OF INTEREST

In taking on financial advisers for a specific assignment, companies should make sure that there is no conflict of interest between the parties. A conflict of interest arose in the LSE–OM merger talks in 2000, with Merrill Lynch resigning as lead financial advisers to the LSE following the publication of an internal report recommending against the merger, leaving the LSE with only one adviser, Salomon Smith Barney.

PRODUCTS AND SERVICES OFFERED

Financial advisers differ in the range of products and services they offer, and in the degree of emphasis on any particular product or service. Some financial advisers may specialize in taking companies to AIM, for example. Others may concentrate on mergers and acquisitions, and/or the raising of finance. A fully-fledged firm such as Goldman Sachs will offer a complete range of financial services on a divisionalized basis. The major commercial and investment banks are also increasingly offering financial advice. Credit Suisse First Boston, for instance, was the fourth largest lead adviser in M&A deals in the first half of 2001, advising on 216 M&A transactions totalling US$ 161 billion (with Goldman Sachs in first place). The big accountancy firms are also very active in corporate finance. It is estimated by a spokesman for Andersen that corporate finance brings in around 5–10 per cent of the company's fees, including income generated from spin-off tax, legal and audit work.

ACCESS TO CAPITAL MARKETS

The financial advisers should be able to raise capital efficiently in the markets and to apply innovative solutions to the structuring of transactions. Access should be available to equity, debt and mezzanine level financing from both in-house and third-party funding sources. Additional areas of expertise the financial advisers should also be able to offer include:

- track record of recent financial successes
- debt and equity placements
- loan facilities
- tax-efficient investments
- trade finance services
- securitization

- interest rate swaps

- public securities purchases, sales and options execution.

GLOBALIZATION OF MARKETS

The increasing globalization of markets is creating a need for a much higher level of international orientation of corporate finance. Finance can be raised not only on the local stock market, but on other international exchanges as well, perhaps by means of dual or multiple listings. Have the financial advisers got the range of services to be able to advise the company in this respect? M&As are increasingly cross-border, again requiring international links to accessible local expertise from the corporate financial advisers.

Accounting principles for IPOs submitted in one country are likely to differ from those in another. Nasdaq, for instance, insists on US-GAAP, whereas European companies have a different standard. The burden falls on the international accountancy advisers to ensure that the two are reconciled.

e-COMMERCE STRATEGIES

e-Business was originally hyped as the future of commerce. The new global click businesses would emerge as the path to profitability. New venture-backed dot.com start-ups went to the market and achieved unbelievable multiples. Traditional valuation techniques had to be revised in coming to grips with new parameters. The new companies sprang up either as start-ups led by enthusiastic entrepreneurs, or as acquisitions by existing companies. Brick and mortar candidates for flotation saw the advantage of adding an e-commerce element to their activities through setting it up themselves or by acquiring one of the new start-ups. Public companies turned to their internet assets and spun them off, thus realizing cash.

Investors went for the high-tech stocks in a big way, and in 2000, the Nasdaq composite index passed the 5000 mark for the first time ever. With the recessionary trends, it subsequently fell back to less than half this value, and even fell below 2000. With the IPO boom in 1999 and early 2000, a lot of new business was generated for the financial advisers. With the downturn, some companies then started to buy back their spin-offs. However, investors objected to the low buy-back prices offered.

Despite the gloom, and profit warnings all over the place, not all internet companies are going to the wall, and as the sector matures, e-commerce is likely to emerge, not as a stand-alone opportunity, but as an essential component of a company's long-term global marketing and sales strategies. The financial sector itself already appears as the major beneficiary of e-commerce, with responsibility for a high percentage of all transactions in value terms. Meanwhile, financial advisers, ready with IT specialists on their staff, and new valuation models, are geared up for further financial advice in the sector once it recovers.

PERSONAL RELATIONSHIPS

Personal relationships nurtured between the corporate financial advisers and their client, often over a number of years, can be important to the client. Besides, such year-long contacts with the same person or persons give the financial advisers a unique insight into the nature of the business and a thorough understanding of strengths as well as weaknesses. Communications and co-operation become easier if personal relationships are strong, and contribute towards making the client feel special. The larger the financial advisers, the greater the risks that senior personnel is transferred to different locations, and the less likelihood there is of forming lasting relationships.

FEES

Fees charged by the financial advisers for their work are difficult to determine in advance, as the advisers cannot with any degree of precision foresee how much work is involved in any particular assignment, especially when it comes to taking a company public or undertaking an M&A deal. Usually, there is a fee payable up-front on signature of a contract or memorandum of understanding, and later fees are worked out on a time/cost basis. The fees may also be incorporated in a complete package, payable in tranches. The financial advisers may take some of their remuneration as an equity stake. This method of remuneration became especially popular with the early highly successful dot.com IPOs such as e-Bay. Some corporate finance companies such as Close Brothers in the UK are prepared to act on a success-related fee basis, with an additional modest retainer fee. However, with many deals not going on to completion, this can be a risky business for the financial advisers.

CONCLUSION

Corporate financial advisers show great diversity in the products and services they have to offer, the way they are operating, the size of their organization, the extent of their expertise, the skill set they have accumulated through practice and experience, and the fees they charge. The reputation of the financial advisers in the marketplace is of particular importance if a company wants to offer securities to the public, not only from the point of view of the investors, but also as far as the broker/dealers are concerned. The selection of corporate financial advisers can be critical for the future success of an organization, and the various factors that combine to make the best choice of corporate financial advisers in any particular case, should therefore be carefully assessed at the highest level.

The top league of professional advisers

OVERVIEW

The UK top league of financial advisers includes securities firms, investment firms, banks, brokers with advisory services, and accountants/auditors. Global financial advisers include Goldman Sachs International, Merrill Lynch, Morgan Stanley, Lehman Brothers and Salomon Smith Barney. The top accountancy firms include Deloitte & Touche Corporate Finance, KPMG, Ernst & Young Corporate Finance, PricewaterhouseCoopers and Andersen. Banks present in London engaged in corporate finance include CSFB, ABM Amro (through Hoare Govett), BNP Paribas, Deutsche Bank, Chase Manhattan, Credit Lyonnais, Dresdner Kleinwort Benson, HSBC Investment Bank, Ing Barings, Nomura International and Rothschild (NM) & Sons.

Well-known financial advisers in the City of London include Cazenoves, Beeson Gregory, Charles Stanley, Close Brothers, Robert Fleming & Co., Hoare Covett, Investec Henderson Crosthwaite, Lazards, Lehman Bros, Williams de Broe, Schroder Salomon Smith Barney, SG Hambros, UBS Warburg, Teather & Greenwood and others.

The big international firms are advisers to corporations around the world. Andersen for instance, was adviser to Philips, the Dutch electronics company, and to Aventis Crop Science on the sale of one of their units to Sumitomo Chemical Co. as well as acting as the sole adviser on the merger of New Zealand Dairy group and Kiwi Cooperative Diaries, and others. Andersen are also consultants and auditors to Enron, the US giant energy group, now embroiled in a major scandal after filing for bankruptcy protection from creditors in December 2001, the biggest ever filing in US history. Softening the blow to Andersen's employees, following the breakup of the global accounting giant, will be the absorption of its national units around the world by one of its key competitors. The proposed merger (March 2002) between KPMG's units outside the US and Andersen's European and Asian entities will be subject to a raft of local regulatory approvals. The envisaged non-cash nature of such a merger will, if approved, create the second largest accounting/auditing firm in the world, after PricewaterhouseCoopers. Advisers to UK-listed firms include UBS Warburg for Sainsbury's, Goldman Sachs and UBS for ICI, Rothschild's for De la Rue, Cazenove for Marks & Spencer, Cazenove and Greenhill & Co. for Cable and Wireless, Cazenove and Merrill Lynch for BT, Merrill Lynch and UBS Warburg for British Airways, and UBS Warburg and Lehman Brothers for Abbey National.

LEAGUE TABLES

Financial advisers

League tables for financial and other professional advisers are compiled by a variety of sources, including Hemscott and Thomson Financial. The league tables rank firms according to the number of clients, total clients' profits and clients with the highest market capitalization. The top ten financial advisers in terms of clients with the highest market capitalization are listed in Table 2.1.

Table 2.1 Clients with the highest market capitalization at fourth quarter 2001

Adviser	£ million
1. Goldman Sachs	351 038.7
2. UBS Warburg Ltd	318 708.2
3. Morgan Stanley	132 605.9
4. Merrill Lynch	119 783.6
5. Lazard Bros	99 255.3
6. Credit Suisse First Boston	95 138.0
7. Cazenove	95 054.6
8. HSBC Investment Bank	93 598.7
9. Schroder Salomon Smith Barney	90 839.0
10. Dresdner Kleinwort Wasserstein	69 788.2

Source: Hemscott plc (2001) website: www.Hemscott.net

IPO underwriters

Table 2.2 lists the top ten underwriters by money raised.

Table 2.2 Underwriter league table by most money raised, January to August 2001

Underwriter	Number of IPOs	Total offering amount (US$ million)
1. Credit Suisse First Boston	15	13 205.5
2. Morgan Stanley Dean Witter	11	12 037.1
3. Salomon Smith Barney	8	9 746.6
4. Goldman, Sachs & Co.	7	3 870.7
5. Merrill Lynch & Co.	12	3 605.0
6. UBS Warburg	3	3 008.3
7. Lehman Brothers	5	1 150.5
8. Deutsche Banc Alex. Brown	4	865.9
9. Banc of America Securities	3	563.6
10. CIBC World Markets	2	357.6

Source: IPO.com, Inc.

Credit Suisse has maintained its position at the top of the league table of IPO underwriters with 15 IPOs until end-August 2001, raising a total of US$ 13 205.5 million. This included the Kraft Foods mega-deal of $8.7 billion.

In second place is Morgan Stanley with 11 deals, raising $12 037.1 million. This figure includes four major IPOs, viz. Agere Systems, Accenture, KPMG Consulting and ADR Statoil, raising a total of $10.2 billion.

Salomon Smith Barney's position was helped by involvement in the Kraft Foods deal, putting them into third place.

Expected to move up the table is Goldman Sachs, with the flotation of the financial services firm Prudential Financial, which is expected to realize around $4 billion.

Mergers and acquisitions

Global M&A activity during the first six months of 2001 was down by US$ 1 trillion from last year. Activity worldwide during the second quarter of 2001 was 44 per cent down on the same period in 2000, with 7300 deals totalling US$ 456.9 billion, 2 per cent up on the first quarter. Signs of stagnation were also evident in the European market, with deals down by half to US$ 326 billion. During the second quarter, 3100 deals of a total of $165 billion were announced, a 6 per cent increase on the previous quarter. The UK was Europe's largest M&A market during the second quarter, with deals amounting to $62.1 billion, followed by Germany ($39.5 billion) and France ($16 billion).

Top deals in Europe included the Allianz/Dresdner Bank merger (US$ 20 billion), the E.On offer for Powergen ($15.7 million) and the Halifax/Bank of Scotland merger of $14.9 billion.

Table 2.3 shows the top five transactions with brokers/equity capital markets (ECM) advisers announced between 1 January and 6 June 2001. The table identifies an advisory role (ECM or equity capital market adviser), which is distinct in some markets from the M&A financial advisory role. In the US, the role defined as ECM broker is largely delivered by the financial adviser.

Table 2.3 Top five transactions with brokers/ECM advisers announced between 1 January and 30 June 2001

Date 2001	Target name	Acquirer name	Rank value (US$ million)	Target broker/ ECM adviser	Acquirer broker/ ECM adviser
1 April	Dresdner Bank AG	Allianz AG	20 594.46		Sal Oppenheimer jr & Cie KGaA
9 April	PowerGen PLC	E.On AG	15 711.43	Dresdner Kleinwort Wasserstein UBS Warburg	Goldman Sachs & Co.
19 March	Billiton Plc	BHP Ltd	15 569.61	JP Morgan Securities Inc. Dresdner Kleinwort Wasserstein	UBS Warburg Australia
4 May	Bank of Scotland Plc	Halifax Group Plc	14 904.44	Cazenovee & Co. Credit Suisse First Boston Int.	Merrill Lynch, Pierce, Fenner
15 Feb.	De Beers Consolidated Mines	DB Investments	10 865.81	HSBC	Merrill Lynch International Cazenove & Co. UBS Warburg

Source: Thomson Financial (2001) website: www.thomsonfinancial.com

Thomson Financial's league tables for announced and completed M&A transactions can be seen in Tables 2.4 and 2.5.

Table 2.4 Worldwide completed mergers and acquisitions for financial advisers for the first half of 2001 compared with the first half of 2000, based on transactions

| Adviser | First half 2001 | | | | First half 2000 | | Percentage |
	Number of deals	Rank	Market share	Rank value $US million	Number of deals	Rank	change in number
Credit Suisse First Boston	219	1	2.0	221 974.3	371	1	–4
KPMG Corporate Finance	186	2	1.7	20 436.3	285	2	–3
JP Morgan	168	3	1.5	222 398.6	283	3	–4
Citigroup/Salomon Smith Barney	167	4	1.5	342 382.4	203	6	–1
Goldman Sachs & Co.	145	5	1.3	536 262.9	206	5	–2
UBS Warburg	142	6	1.3	101 192.7	138	9	
Morgan Stanley	124	7	1.1	342 943.2	226	4	–4
Merrill Lynch & Co. Inc.	120	8	1.1	381 649.1	155	8	–2
Deutsche Bank AG	103	9	.9	51 215.0	124	10	–1
PricewaterhouseCoopers	94	10	.9	6 906.3	169	7	–4
Rothchild	84	11	.8	74 880.8	104	12	–1
Lehman Brothers	80	12	.7	77 188.4	116	11	–3
Lazard	73	13	.7	90 554.2	97	15	–24
ABN AMRO	67	14	.6	17 593.5	89	16	–24
Ernst & Young LLP	63	15	.6	3 897.8	98	14	–35
Arthur Andersen	61	16	.6	3 949.3	101	13	–39
Mizuho Financial Group	48	17	.4	8 698.8	32	36	50
Grant Thornton LLP	47	18	.4	1 249.7	67	19	–29
CIBC World Markets	47	18	.4	51 350.2	54	25	–12
Societe Generale	45	20	.4	18 249.7	72	18	–37
BNP Paribas SA	41	21	.4	15 526.4	49	27	–16
Deloitte & Touche LLP	40	22	.4	3 382.8	60	22	–33
Houlihan Lokey Howard & Zukin	40	22	.4	16 091.3	66	20	–39
Nippo Securities Co. Ltd	40	22	.4	1 182.5	34	35	17
Dresdner Kleinwort Wasserstein	39	25	.4	264 578.4	78	17	–50
Deals with adviser	2 310	–	21.0	1 098 299.3	3 568	–	–35
Deals without adviser	8 681	–	79.0	87 583.2	11 501	–	–24
Industry totals	10 991	–	100.0	1 185 882.5	15 069	–	–27

Source: Thomson Financial (973) 622-3100 07/03/2001

Table 2.5 Worldwide announced mergers and acquisitions for financial advisers for the first half of 2001, compared with the first half of 2000, based on rank value

Adviser	First half 2001				First half 2000		Percentage
	Rank value $US million	Rank	Market share	Number of deals	Rank value $US million	Rank	change in rank value
Goldman Sachs & Co.	253 850.8	1	28.0	166	740 749.7	2	−65.73
Merrill Lynch & Co. Inc.	200 146.5	2	22.1	119	492 008.1	4	−59.32
Morgan Stanley	198 225.7	3	21.9	135	848 772.0	1	−76.65
Credit Suisse First Boston	161 051.3	4	17.8	216	499 572.0	3	−67.76
JP Morgan	152 605.4	5	16.8	189	289 911.5	7	−47.36
Citigroup/Salomon Smith Barney	120 657.4	6	13.3	184	477 935.5	5	−74.75
UBS Warburg	117 817.5	7	13.0	135	244 441.2	8	−51.80
Dresdner Kleinwort Wasserstein	107 982.6	8	11.9	44	314 160.1	6	−65.63
Deutsche Bank AG	74 726.1	9	8.3	112	72 184.3	13	3.52
Rothschild	68 902.1	10	7.6	78	104 557.9	11	−34.10
Lehman Brothers	60 151.8	11	6.6	74	156 444.2	9	−61.55
Lazard	40 523.0	12	4.5	72	148 580.8	10	−72.73
Greenhill & Co., LLC	31 291.4	13	3.5	12	38 982.0	17	−19.73
Sal Oppenheim Jr & Cie KGaA	25 324.5	14	2.8	10	−	309	
Societe Generale	23 420.7	15	2.6	44	30 499.5	21	−23.21
Gresham Partners	18 348.5	16	2.0	6	45.8	234	39 962.23
CIBC World Markets	17 984.4	17	2.0	54	23 562.5	25	−23.67
Cazenove & Co.	16 932.1	18	1.9	14	44 561.9	15	−62.00
Bear Stearns & Co. Inc.	15 965.7	19	1.8	46	34 425.8	19	−53.62
BNP Paribas SA	15 195.8	20	1.7	38	8 051.7	38	88.73
Gleacher & Co. LLC	14 904.4	21	1.6	1	14 396.1	32	3.53
ABN AMRO	14 560.7	22	1.6	62	40 324.3	16	−63.89
Grant Samuel & Associates Pty	11 616.7	23	1.3	8	6 686.1	44	73.74
Enskilda Securities	11 121.5	24	1.2	18	12 421.6	33	−10.47
Banc of America Securities LLC	11 075.5	25	1.2	29	33 629.5	20	−67.07
Deals with adviser	779 542.9	−	86.0	2 521	1 771 178.4	−	−55.99
Deals without adviser	126 558.1	−	14.0	12 767	172 354.6	−	−26.57
Industry totals	906 100.9	−	100.0	15 288	1 943 533.0	−	−53.38

Source: Thomson Financial (973) 622-3100 07/03/2001

Table 2.6 shows the UK public target financial advisers league table ranked by value of deals completed and withdrawn 1 January to 30 June 2001.

Table 2.6 UK public target financial advisers league table ranked by value of deals completed and withdrawn 1 January to 30 June 2001

Adviser	No. of deals	Value (£ million)
1. JP Morgan	4	15 301
2. Citigroup/Salomon Smith Barney	8	12 520
3. Dresdner Kleinwort Wasserstein	6	11 966
4. UBS Warburg	4	11 690
5. Gresham Partners	1	10 892
6. Rothschild	8	7 489
7. Morgan Stanley	9	7 283
8. Lazard	10	7 061
9. Credit Suisse First Boston	6	6 883
10. Lehman Brothers	4	6 273
11. Goldman Sachs & Co.	2	4 897
12. Deutsche Bank AG	5	2 000
13. ABN AMRO	3	1 436
14. Close Brothers	3	1 327
15. KPMG Corporate Finance	7	925
16. Cazenove & Co.	2	722
17. ING Barings	2	482
18. Robert W. Baird & Co.	2	451
19. Noble Grossart	1	399
20. Deloitte & Touche	3	301

Source: Thomson Financial (2001) website: www.thomsonfinancial.com

Stockbrokers

In terms of stockbroking, the ranking is shown in Table 2.7.

Table 2.7 Clients with the highest market capitalization at fourth quarter 2001 (stockbrokers)

Adviser	£ million
1. Cazenove	532 385.55
2. UBS Warburg	420 636.60
3. Merrill Lynch	341 167.30
4. Hoare Govett	324 206.45
5. Credit Suisse First Boston (Europe)	318 170.05
6. Goldman Sachs Equity Securities (UK)	125 500.30
7. HSBC	117 017.90
8. Dresdner Kleinwort Wasserstein	64 472.00
9. Schroder Salomon Smith Barney	57 597.30
10. Deutsche Bank AG (London)	53 848.70

Source: Hemscott plc (2001) website: www.Hemscott.net

Accountancy firms

Also acting as corporate finance advisers are the big international accountancy firms, Deloitte & Touche Corporate Finance, KPMG Corporate Finance, Andersen, PricewaterhouseCoopers and Ernst & Young. The accountancy firms are invariably involved in major takeovers and flotations. They may be accountants and auditors to the companies in the first place, but if a company already has local accountants, it may be necessary also to bring in a big firm of accountants to succeed in a flotation.

■ Deloitte & Touche corporate finance division advises corporate clients, including private firms and governments. Disciplines include accounting, banking, and broking and consulting, bringing to a deal experience in acquisitions, disposals, private equity, transactional services, valuations, public/private partnerships and project finance. The corporate finance division of Deloitte and Touche has some 250 staff in the UK and 440 employees in Europe. Globally, the company specializes in the techs, media and telecoms (TMT) and healthcare sectors, but also serves other sectors.

A record overall revenue growth of 19.3 per cent was announced for the year ended May 2001, of £822 million, up from £689 million last year. Overall financial services performed well during the fiscal year, but there was a slowdown in M&A activity towards the latter part of the year. Major clients included the Royal Bank of Scotland Group (audit).

■ Ernst & Young was awarded the 'Big Five Firm of the Year' award for 2001 by *Accountancy Age*. It is one of the largest professional services firms in the United Kingdom. Half of the 460 partners and 6500 staff work in London. The firm has offices in a further 19 locations worldwide.

Corporate clients include multinationals (Amex, BP Amoco, British Airways, Coca-Cola, Electrolux, Ford, UBS and Wal-Mart).

Major UK companies include Abbey National, BBC, Boots and Lloyds of London.

e-Business clients include amazon.com and Netstore.

The firm reported a 22 per cent increase in corporate finance fees for 2000, a growth of 15 per cent in taxation services and 14 per cent in business assurance.

Ernst & Young also runs what it claims to be 'the most interactive (website) portal of the Big Five'.

■ Grant Thornton is a major US accounting financial adviser providing accounting and auditing services as well as tax consulting and corporate finance. They employ more than 20 000 people in over 100 countries.

The league table of accountants/auditors in Table 2.8 shows the ranking of the big five in terms of clients' market capitalization.

Table 2.8 Clients with the highest market capitalization at fourth quarter 2001 (accountants/auditors)

Adviser	£ million
1. PricewaterhouseCoopers	608 479.9
2. KPMG	320 431.1
3. Deloitte Touche	245 111.9
4. Ernst & Young	199 476.7
5. Arthur Andersen	69 941.6
6. Grant Thornton	4 249.4
7. BDO Stoy Hayward	4 019.9
8. RSM Robson Rhodes	1 956.7
9. Baker Tilly	1 606.0
10. Binder Hamlyn	922.1

Source: Hemscott plc (2001) website: www.Hemscott.net

Law firms

Law firms involved in deal structuring include Denton Wilde Sapte (awarded first place in *Euromoney's* trade finance awards for excellence 2000) and Clifford Chance.

Denton Wilde Sapte counts among its clients the Bank of Scotland, Dixons, Easyjet and Sainsbury's. Their experience in corporate work enables them to advise on cross border mergers, acquisitions, disposals and joint ventures. Specialists in taxation, intellectual property and other aspects of transactions are available.

Denton Wilde Sapte are experienced in corporate transactions in all sectors and has expertise in the financing of joint ventures. They also advise on exit strategies and due diligence.

Clifford Chance advises on large, complex M&A transactions. With offices in Europe, America and Asia, Clifford Chance has the largest corporate practice of any firm of legal advisers, with a broad range of clients, including companies and public corporations, investment banks and other financial institutions, governments and international organizations. Worldwide, Clifford Chance ranked fourth in terms of value of M&A transactions and second by volume in Thomson Financial Securities tables during the first half of 2001. Their corporate finance has special expertise in advising on competition issues in M&As, joint ventures and strategic alliances, and also advise on IPOs and shareholder disputes. In private equity, they advise on MBOs, MBIs and leveraged buy-outs. They also advise many financial institutions, including banks, brokers, insurance companies, fund managers, investment banks and stock exchanges.

Hemscott's league table for legal advisers is shown in Table 2.9.

Table 2.9 Clients with the highest market capitalization at fourth quarter 2001 (legal advisers)

Adviser	£ million
1. Linklater & Alliance	559 808.0
2. Slaughter & May	304 331.5
3. Allen & Overy	192 238.6
4. Freshfields Bruckhaus Deringer	162 879.8
5. Norton Rose	89 743.0
6. Herbert Smith	81 799.1
7. Ashurst Morris Crisp	61 377.8
8. Clifford Chance	60 086.5
9. Rowe & Maw	58 739.8
10. Field Fisher Waterhouse	54 621.6

Source: Hemscott plc (2001) website: www.Hemscott.net

The International Centre for Commercial Law has issued a league table of London-based law firms in terms of numbers of fee-earners per firm. This is shown in Table 2.10.

Table 2.10 Law firms listed by number of fee earners in the London region

1. Clifford Chance LLP	1342
2. Linklaters	1127
3. Freshfields Bruckhaus Deringer	1093
4. Allen & Overy	1070
5. Lovells	769
6. Herbert Smith	727
7. Norton Rose	625
8. CMS Cameron McKenna	618
9. Denton Wilde Sapte	611
10. Ashurst Morris Crisp	570

Source: The International Centre for Commercial Law (2002) *The UK Legal 500 – the client's guide to UK law firms*. Tel 020 7396 9313.

The league table of UK firms with worldwide fee-earners is shown in Table 2.11.

Table 2.11 UK law firms listed by number of worldwide fee-earners

1. Evershed	1624
2. Clifford Chance LLP	1342
3. DLA	1212
4. Linklaters	1127
5. Freshfields Bruckhaus Deringer	1093
6. Allen & Overy	1070
7. Hammond Suddards Edge	825
8. Lovells	769
9. Herbert Smith	727
10. Addleshaw Booth & Co.	689

Source: The International Centre for Commercial Law (2002) *The UK Legal 500 – the client's guide to UK law firms*.

US law firms

The ten practices of US law firms active in corporate finance in London top the list of US firms published by *The UK Legal 500*, The International Centre for Commercial Law, but there are no comparative figures in terms of number of fee-earners. They are as follows:

Cleary, Gottlieb, Steen & Hamilton

Cravath, Swaine & Moore's

Davis Polk & Wardwell

Shearman & Sterling

Simpson Thacher & Bartlett

Skadden, Arps, Slate, Meagher & Flom LLP

Sullivan & Cromwell

Weil, Gotshal & Manges

Brobeck, Hale & Dorr

Cadwalader, Wickersham & Taft.

The firms have all been involved in some impressive international deals. Cleary, Gottlieb, Steen & Hamilton, for instance, represented Robert Fleming & Co. when it was acquired by Chase Manhattan in a £4.8 billion deal, and was also involved in HSBC Holdings' purchase of Credit Commercial de France (£6.6 billion).

Cravath, Swaine & Moore's represented Marconi when it first listed in the US. Davis Polk & Wardwell was involved in more than 80 M&A transactions in Europe during 2000. Approximately the same number of deals were consummated in Europe by Shearman & Sterling (including the Glaxo Welcome/SmithKlein Beecham deal). Simpson Thacher & Bartlett were active in several European acquisitions in the US, notably UBS AG's taking over of Paine Webber Group. Skadden, Arps, Slate, Meagher & Flom are expanding in Europe. Sullivan & Cromwell advised on the mega MeritaNordbanken's acquisition of the Danish Unibank ($4.7 billion). Weil, Gotshal & Manges were also involved in major deals, including the Flextech/Telewest merger. Brobeck, Hale & Dorr have specialized in high-tech deals (venture capital and M&As). Cadwalader, Wickersham & Taft count among their top clients Morgan Stanley Dean Witter and Barclays.

Thomson Financial provides a league table (*see* Table 2.12) for US legal advisers involved in M&As, based on rank value.

Table 2.12 US legal advisers involved in mergers and acquisitions, based on rank value

Adviser	First half 2001				First half 2000		Percentage change in number
	Number of deals	Rank	Market share	Rank value $US million	Number of deals	Rank	
Jones Day Reavis & Pogue	125	1	4.0	230 755.7	124	1	0.81
Dorsey & Whitney LLP	116	2	3.7	5 389.3	122	2	−4.92
Gibson Dunn & Crutcher	75	3	2.4	33 388.9	88	4	−14.77
Skadden, Arps, Slate, Meagher & Flom	57	4	1.8	241 344.6	83	6	−31.33
Wilson Sonsini Goodrich & Rosati	55	5	1.7	51 925.8	113	3	−51.33
Sullivan & Cromwell	53	6	1.7	368 995.8	71	7	−25.35
Dewey Ballantine LLP	47	7	1.5	281 310.8	70	8	−32.86
Weil Gotshal & Manges	45	8	1.4	30 405.0	35	23	28.57
Morris Nichols Arsht & Tunnell	40	9	1.3	83 540.1	42	19	−4.76
Gray Cary Ware & Freidenrich	38	10	1.2	2 296.9	39	21	−2.56
Brobeck Phleger & Harrison LLP	38	10	1.2	7 927.5	86	5	−55.81
Shearman & Sterling	37	12	1.2	70 703.4	56	10	−33.93
Wachtell Lipton Rosen & Katz	35	13	1.1	122 246.2	43	17	−18.60
Latham & Watkins	34	14	1.1	24 436.7	50	13	−32.00
Simpson Thacher & Bartlett	31	15	1.0	249 623.2	62	9	−50.00
Cooley Godward LLP	31	15	1.0	2 573.3	48	14	−35.42
Sidley Austin Brown & Wood	27	17	.9	52 776.8	45	16	−40.00
Cleary Gottlieb Steen & Hamilton	27	17	.9	260 562.6	32	24	−15.63
Baker Botts LLP	25	19	.8	22 032.6	43	17	−41.86
Cravath, Swaine & Moore	24	20	.8	232 166.0	27	27	−11.11
Arnold & Porter	23	21	.7	8 034.5	26	28	−11.54
Fried Frank Harris Shriver & Jacobson	23	21	.7	92 004.6	36	22	−36.11
Bryan Cave LLP	22	23	.7	182 234.0	52	12	−57.69
Clifford Chance	20	24	.6	16 364.7	11	37	81.82
Davis Polk & Wardwell	18	25	.6	45 577.2	55	11	−67.27
Deals with legal advisers	889	–	28.2	582 606.7	1372	–	−35.20
Deals w/o legal adv (incl in-house)	2265	–	71.9	66 774.4	3429	–	−33.95
Industry totals	3152	–	100.0	649 325.0	4792	–	−34.22

Source: Thomson Financial (973) 622-3100 07/03/2001

Public relations/investor relations firms

Public relations advisers have become essential in the promotion of IPOs and M&As, and in maintaining investor interest and public awareness in the longer term.

In recent years, the visibility of mergers and acquisitions has grown enormously in terms of media exposure and interest. The amount of coverage of deals in the world press has increased exponentially. Anthony Payne, Managing Director of the United States PR firm Hill & Knowlton Financial Division, illustrates this trend with figures: in 1995, there were some 500 articles covering the subject; in 2000, there were 20 000. Anthony Payne said that one reason for this is that the M&A market itself has grown, but nowhere near at the same rate as the media coverage.

An area that has shown particular growth is the cross-border M&A market, especially since the advent of the EU Single Market, and as far as cross-border deals are concerned, Hill & Knowlton is in pole position, due to its size and global structure. Hill & Knowlton rank second in the world in terms of overall financial PR work.

As media interest has grown, so has the influence of the media. Partly due to this, political interest and involvement has also grown, and more attention is focused on the analysts who are becoming media commentators in their own right. Shareholders and investors have to be kept informed of the deal as it progresses, and be persuaded to do what is in their company's best interest. The same applies to the employees and the unions.

For all these reasons, communications experts are required. The financial advisers or the companies themselves are there to structure the deal and bring together an expert team, and are likely to assist in advising on press releases and disclosure of information to the stock exchange; but when it comes to explaining a deal in terms of managing stories through the press, and sending out circulars and diagrams, the actual crafting is left to the PR consultants. Advertising and arranging roadshows also fall within their remit.

A large-scale IPO involves professional advisers spanning from financial advisers, bankers, legal experts, accountants and specialists such as trade mark agents and valuation experts, and invariably creates a high communications component. The audience consists not only of those immediately involved, such as investors, shareholders, and employees, but also the company's customers, and the wider general public and interest groups.

The PR firms have responded to this need, and have developed teams of high levels of expertise. Hill & Knowlton, for instance has its own design group, a political group, and experts on financial technology. Hill & Knowlton rank second in the world in terms of overall financial PR work. Its financial services team is responsible for transactions such as M&As and IPOs.

Like the financial advisers, the PR firms have developed sector expertise, such as healthcare, biotechnology and IT. Some PR companies specialize in taking small companies to AIM, such as Buchanan Communications and SquareMile.

The number of PR firms with M&A expertise is limited, estimated at some 50, and those with international expertise are very few indeed. In the financial sector, the corporate financial advisers and investment banks are the most important providers of PR business.

The league table of financial PR advisers in the UK is shown in Table 2.13.

Table 2.13 Clients with the highest market capitalization at fourth quarter 2001 (financial PR advisers)

Financial PR adviser	£ million
1. Financial Dynamics	210 471.5
2. Brunswick	188 367.7
3. Tavistock Communications	111 846.8
4. Finsbury	110 898.1
5. Maitland Consultancy	91 512.1
6. The Wriglesworth Consultancy	44 762.0
7. Citigate Dewe Rogerson	42 548.7
8. Bell Pottinger Financial	37 308.7
9. Hogarth	33 556.4
10. Gavin Andersen & Co.	27 806.8

Source: Hemscott plc (2001) website: www.Hemscott.net

Other financial PR firms well known in the City include Weber Shandwick Worldwide, Buchanan Communications and Square Mile BSMG.

Other professional advisers include specialists on valuation, real estate, intellectual property, actuarial and insurance. Such specialists are drawn upon as and when required, depending on the particular needs of any one organization.

CONCLUSION

The top league of corporate financial advisers are fiercely proud of earning the top position in the various ranking tables that are published by commercial organizations such as Hemscott and Thomson Financial. If the advisers are near the top, they will publish it on their website for all to see, or incorporate it in their capability statements which are handed out to clients for promotional and assessment purposes. The tables also act as a motivational force. Those professional advisers that are at the top of the league, will strive to remain there, those that follow, will work harder to move higher. From the clients' point of view, the rankings will provide them with a choice of advisers according to criteria that may be relevant, such as M&A deal size, or number of IPOs. The tables also allow clients to compare the relative position of the various advisers, and even use a particular ranking as a bargaining point in negotiating over fees.

Corporate financial advisers in the United States

OVERVIEW

The largest financial services firms are US-based, typically with headquarters in New York. Many of the firms had offices in the WTC and adjoining buildings, including Goldman Sachs, Morgan Stanley, Merrill Lynch, Lehman Brothers and others, and suffered severe setbacks from the murderous attacks on 11 September, with an appalling loss of life, including 64 British citizens, and a total destruction of physical assets and offices.

Worst hit was Cantor Fitzgerald who lost their top dealers among the 540 staff dead and missing. Keefe Bruyette & Woods lost 67 out of 220 employees, including top analysts. Morgan Stanley suffered relatively modest losses with the collapse of the two buildings in the complex where they had offices.

ECONOMIC OUTLOOK

11 September 2001 happened at the worst possible time for the world economy. A slowdown was already under way before the disaster, and was soon heading towards recession with the shockwaves pounding through not only the US economy, but the global economy as a whole. Central banks, financial institutions and other commentators downgraded their economic growth forecasts. CEBR lowered its forecast for 2002 for world GDP to 2.2 per cent in the wake of the attack. Profits warnings flooded the market, led by the likes of Merrill Lynch, Goldman Sachs and Morgan Stanley. Stock markets faltered, and interim company results showed plunging revenues. Investors turned to bonds and hedge funds, or stopped investing altogether. The gold price rose briefly, but with a return of the markets to pre-11 September levels, fell back again.

The financial services industry faced a severe decline in business. Activity in capital markets slowed down, mergers and acquisitions business started to dry up and IPOs were withdrawn or postponed. Corporate valuations became uncertain, due to the volatility in the stock market, acting as a further brake on M&A deals.

Although badly hit, stock markets picked up slowly over the coming months. Pre-11 September, there had already been talk of recession, but the attacks triggered Wall Street to drastically plunge to new lows, as shares lost US$ 1.4 trillion in the ensuing week. London, Paris, Frankfurt and Amsterdam all fell, with the FTSE 100 plunging more than a third from its 1999 high. Tokyo also suffered, partly due to poor trade figures, and Hong Kong dropped sharply. Insurers and re-insurers were also under pressure, with estimates of payouts in the billions. Munich estimated claims to be around € 2.1 billion, and Swiss Re, € 2 billion. Prudential Financial, about to go public, expected to pay out claims for around US$ 400 million related to the WTC annihilation. The finance industry announced the shedding of thousands of jobs as brokers turned to safe haven investments and hedge funds. Defence stocks went up, as the Pentagon went to war.

The UK, seemingly sheltered from the worst effects of the US slowdown, also felt the aftermath of the attacks, particularly in the airline industry. With passenger deserting the airlines in droves, the airline companies came under pressure, and announced cuts in routes, revision of aircraft orders, selling off of aircraft and massive layoffs. British Airways and Virgin Atlantic, losing transatlantic business, announced layoffs of 1000s, whilst the low-cost airlines increased their market share. Other airlines across Europe were also in difficulties. SwissAir, regarded as the most stable of airlines, ran into problems, and the Swiss Government had to step in to prevent immediate collapse. Sabena declared itself bankrupt. Following interest rate cuts in the US, the Bank of England cut rates to their lowest levels for decades. American Airlines, whose two aircraft had been used as manned missiles aimed at the WTC, suffered a further blow with the crash in New York on 12 November of yet another of their aircraft.

LAYOFFS

The inevitable consolidation and belt tightening led to massive job losses in financial services. Estimates put job losses globally at around 30 000. Even before 11 September, investment firms had started laying off staff. Morgan Stanley and Goldman Sachs between them cut more than 2000 jobs in the spring. In May 2001, ABM AMRO cut hundreds of jobs from its global equities business and administrative staff. Salomon Smith Barney announced a 10 per cent cut in investment banking, or some 300 people. This was part of parent Citigroup's plan to phase out some 3500 jobs. PricewaterhouseCooper earmarked some 300 consultants for voluntary redundancy, but this could be attributed to the recent merger between PW and Coopers. KPMG announced plans to cut staff by up to 400 people in the UK, and cut staff in the US. Credit Suisse First Boston cut jobs, as did UBS Warburg, Deutsche Bank, Ing Baring and others.

GLOBAL REACH

Over the years, the financial advisers have spread their network worldwide, and typically have offices in all major financial centres, including London, Paris, Frankfurt, Tokyo, Hong Kong, Singapore and Zurich. Morgan Stanley, for instance, has offices in some 28 major cities around the world.

The fully-fledged organization of the large institutions offers a multitude of financial products and services. Some of the main players' performance and strategies are outlined below.

Morgan Stanley Dean Witter

Morgan Stanley Dean Witter reported net income of US$ 735 million for the quarter ended 31 August 2001, compared with the same period last year of US$ 1246 million. For the first nine months of fiscal year 2001, net income was US$ 2740 million, compared with last year's US$ 4248 million. Third quarter net revenues were US$ 5271 million, down from US$ 6309 million in 2000.

Announcing the results, Morgan Stanley expressed concern regarding the global economic outlook, but viewed long-term growth opportunities with a degree of optimism.

It extended its worldwide reach with the merger of the two entities Dean Witter, Discover & Co. and Morgan Stanley Group Inc. in 1997. The Group's network comprises some 60 000 employees and more than 700 offices in 28 countries.

Morgan Stanley has recently experienced increased competition from commercial banks, insurance companies and other financial service providers.

The company is organized into three segments: securities, asset management and credit services. The securities business includes corporate finance activities such as mergers and acquisitions, restructuring, project finance and real estate, as well as underwriting and trading. The company has also created an on-line brokerage service. They were co-founders of Jiway together with the OM Group, but later pulled out of the deal. In addition, research services are provided, as well as commodities trading and foreign exchange. Securities lending, derivatives and private equity activities are also part of their business. The asset management business advises on portfolio management. Credit Services runs a credit card called Discover and the Morgan Stanley Dean Witter card as well as a proprietary network of cash access locations.

Morgan Stanley's revenues from its investment banking business in 2001 are shown in Table 3.1.

To promote their investment offerings, Morgan Stanley's investment arm is in partnerships with other well-known providers of financial providers, including Charles Schwab, JP Morgan, Invesco, Mellon/Dreyfus, PricewaterhouseCoopers/Kwasha Lipton and Wells Fargo.

Table 3.1 Morgan Stanley: revenues from investment banking business in 2001

Morgan Stanley Dean Witter & Company – Financial information and statistical data – (unaudited)

	30 Nov 2001	30 Nov 2000	31 Aug 2001	Percentage change from: 30 Nov 2000	31 Aug 2001
Morgan Stanley					
Total Assets (millions)	$ 484 000	$ 427 000	$ 507 000	13%	(5%)
Period end common shares outstanding (millions)	1 093.0	1 107.3	1 106.3	(1%)	(1%)
Book value per common share	$ 18.64	16.91	$ 17.76	10%	5%
Shareholders' equity (millions) (1)	$ 21 926	$ 19 671	$ 21 199	11%	3%
Total capital (millions) (2)	$ 61 633	$ 49 637	$ 60 652	24%	2%
Worldwide employees	61 319	62 679	62 392	(2%)	(2%)
SECURITIES					
Advisory revenue (millions)	$ 319	$ 566	$ 360	(44%)	(11%)
Underwriting revenue (millions)	$ 479	$ 542	$ 417	(12%)	15%
Institutional Securities					
Sales and trading net revenue (millions) (3)	$ 1 392	$ 1 436	$ 1 778	(3%)	(22%)
Mergers and acquisitions announced transactions (4)					
Morgan Stanley global market volume (billions)	$ 395.0	$ 1 069.5	$ 279.4		
Rank	3	2	4		
Worldwide equity and related issues (4)					
Morgan Stanley global market volume (billions)	$ 40.2	$ 59.3	$ 32.9		
Rank	4	3	4		
Individual Investor Group					
Net revenue (millions)	$ 986	$ 1 276	$ 1 056	(23%)	(7%)
Global financial advisers	13 690	13 966	14 342	(2%)	(5%)
Total client assets (billions)	$ 595	$ 662	$ 597	(10%)	–
Fee-based client account (billions) (5)	$ 110	$ 121	$ 109	(9%)	1%
INVESTMENT MANAGEMENT ($ billions)					
Assets under management or supervision					
Products offered primarily to individuals					
Mutual funds					
Equity	$ 83	$ 103	$ 85	(19%)	(2%)
Fixed income	36	46	41	(22%)	(12%)
Money markets	66	57	65	16%	2%
Total mutual funds	185	206	191	(10%)	(3%)
ICS Assets	30	31	31	(3%)	(3%)
Separate accounts, unit trust and other arrangements	65	78	70	(17%)	(7%)
Sub-total individual	280	315	292	(11%)	(4%)
Products offered primarily to institutional clients					
Mutual funds	38	35	38	9%	–
Separate accounts, pooled vehicle and other arrangements	141	150	141	(6%)	–
Sub-total institutional	179	185	179	(3%)	–
Total assets under management or supervision	$ 459	$ 500	$ 471	(8%)	(3%)

(1) Includes preferred and common equity and preferred securities issued by subsidiaries.

(2) Includes preferred and common equity, preferred securities issued by subsidiaries, capital units and non-current portion of long-term debt.

(3) Includes principal trading, commissions and net interest revenue.

(4) Source: Thomson Financial Securities Data – 1 January to 30 November 2001.

(5) Represents the amount of assets in client accounts where the basis of payment for services is a fee calculated on those assets.

Source: Morgan Stanley press release (2001)

Merrill Lynch

One of the firms that lost their headquarters on 11 September, Merrill Lynch is another giant in the financial services industry. The company prides itself on 'unlocking value' for its investors, clients and shareholders through strategic leverage of their critical resources. Their leverage operation is driven by client relationships. Intellectual growth and technology leadership in global financial markets has been achieved in investments across the world.

Operating results for the first nine months and third quarter of 2001 are shown in Table 3.2.

Table 3.2 Merrill Lynch: operating results for the first nine months and third quarter of 2001

dollars in millions	3rdQ 01	9 mths 01
Net revenues (millions)	$5125	$17 128
Net earnings (millions)	$422(1)	$1 837(1)

(1) Includes $53 million after-tax of 11 September related expenses ($88 million pre-tax)

Source: Merrill Lynch (2002)

The company has three main segments: corporate and institutional finance, private clients and investment management. Their research team is 900 strong across 26 countries in the world, and includes economists and analysts. Merrill Lynch is strong in the technology sector, and technological change has been supported through investments in technological innovation.

Merrill Lynch has handled transactions for some of the world's largest telecommunications companies, including AT&T Wireless, British Telecom, NTT and China Mobile.

International business

The Group has provided financing for Solectron on its acquisition of Natsteel Electronics (Singapore), and they managed the largest-ever convertible bond issue (US$ 3.45 billion) for Tyco International. They were joint leader for a large equity placement for Brazilian Petrobras and advised a German client, RWE, on the acquisition of Britain's Thames Water.

Goldman Sachs

Goldman Sachs offers financial services on a worldwide basis. Its activities are divided into two main segments, global capital markets, and asset management and securities services.

The company ranked first in Thomson Financial Services market sector analysis on announced mergers and acquisitions during 2001 in terms of value (US$ 138 370 million) with Morgan Stanley in second place (US$ 117 717 million). Global capital markets are subdivided into investment banking and trading and principal investments.

Investment banking activities comprise financial advisory and underwriting. Advisory assignments include mergers and acquisitions, divestitures, corporate defence activities, restructuring and spinoffs. Underwriting includes public offerings and private placements.

Trading and principal investments fall into three categories: fixed income, currency and commodities; equities; and principal investments.

Asset management consists of investment advisory services. Securities services include brokerage-financing services and securities lending as well as matched book business.

Commissions include securities and options clearing services.

Organization structure

Figure 3.1 summarizes the activities carried out by Goldman Sachs.

Fig. 3.1 Activities carried out by Goldman Sachs

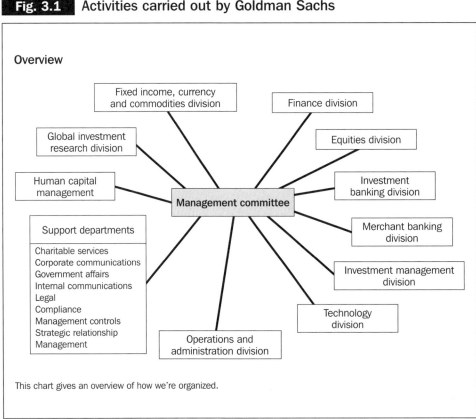

Source: Goldman Sachs (2002)

International activities

In investment banking, Goldman Sachs is the No. 1 global underwriter of IPOs (2000), and they advised on seven out of ten of the largest mergers in the world (deal value US$ 1.3 trillion). Their own IPO passed more than 55 per cent of the firm to employees. More than 40 per cent of net revenue was contracted by their European and Asian operations.

Goldman Sachs acted as financial advisers to state-controlled Repsol in its two-step US$ 16 billion acquisition of YPF in 1999. This was the largest cash transaction in the energy sector, the largest cross-border transaction by a Spanish company and the largest acquisition in Latin America.

The company also acted as an adviser to the US$ 34 billion merger between Zeneca Group Plc and Astra AB of Sweden, in the largest pharmaceutical merger ever. Astra Zeneca plc is one of the leading global pharmaceutical companies.

Swiss Reinsurance company was assisted by Goldman Sachs in raising capital through their 'triple play' exchangeable bond. The offering raised some US$ 530 million at a premium of 40 per cent.

Goldman Sachs were also lead manager and adviser to the flotation of China Telecom in 1997 when US$ 4.2 billion was raised, and later advised China Telecom on further acquisitions, and an equity offering of US$ 2 billion.

They acted as financial advisers to Vodaphone's merger with Airtouch (US$ 12.5 billion), as well as being lead manager in RedHat's successful US$ 96.6 million IPO.

Lehman Brothers

Founded in 1850, Lehman Brothers are leaders in equity and fixed income trading, investment banking, private equity and private clients services. Their headquarters at the World Finance Centre, adjacent to the World Trade Centre, was evacuated on 11 September, and they have subsequently announced an agreement to purchase Morgan Stanley's new 1 million square-foot office block on Seventh Avenue. Morgan Stanley's own head office of 1.4 million square-foot is in Broadway.

Lehman Brothers 'One Firm' approach relies on bringing together resources from all divisions in the service of their clients. The firm focuses on a range of activities:

■ The global economics team, from New York, Tokyo and London, analyzes key economic variables and their effects of markets in more than 50 countries.

■ The credit risk management division provides advice to facilitate clients' transactions, and undertakes due diligence assignments. Suitable credit policies and guidelines are recommended.

■ The fixed income division. In fixed income, Lehman Brothers managed a total of US$ 2.4 billion in high-yield securities, and served as lead manager for over

US$ 2.7 billion mortgage-backed insurance and US$ 30 billion of asset-backed placements (2000).

■ The asset backed placements division. Lehman Brothers is the sole arranger for a US$ 1.5 billion transaction, for Zurich Capital Markets, issued by Lehman Brothers' structured trust programme.

■ The equities division. Net revenues from equities reached US$ 2.6 billion during 2000. Lehman Brothers lead managed 100 equity and equity-related deals in 2000, totalling more than US$ 20 billion. Of Lehman's equity and equity-related underwriting volume, 37 per cent was issued internationally.

Lehman Brothers provides banking and investment banking services internationally, and has recently set up a website.

In investment banking, Lehman Brothers employs some 1200 investment bankers in 28 offices in 21 countries worldwide, and provides advisory and capital raising services. It works closely with the private equity division, which has total committed capital of US$ 5 billion.

MAGNITUDE OF STOCK MARKETS SERVED BY FINANCIAL ADVISERS

The magnitude of the markets served by the financial advisers is illustrated by a comparison between the main stock markets and the number of companies listed (*see* Table 3.3). The US is by far the largest market, but London and Tokyo are also well represented.

Table 3.3 Number of companies with shares listed on main markets

Exchange	Total year 2000 (excluding investment funds)
Amex	649
Nasdaq	4734
NYSE	2862
Toronto	1421
Canadian Venture Exchange	2598
Deutsche Borse	989
London	2374
Euronext Amsterdam	392
Euronext Paris	966
Euronext Brussels	265

Exchange	Total year 2000 (excluding investment funds)
Madrid	1036
Australian	1406
Hong Kong	790
Osaka	1310
Tokyo	2096

Source: FIBV Annual Report 2000

CLIENTS OF US FINANCIAL INSTITUTIONS

Clients of the US financial services institutions are the world's largest companies. The ten largest companies in terms of revenue are listed in Table 3.4. More than half of them are listed on NYSE.

Table 3.4 Ten largest companies in terms of revenue for 2000

Company	Revenues (US$ million) 2000
Exxon Mobil Co.	210 392
WalMart Stores Inc.	193 295
General Motors	164 632
Ford Motor Co.	180 598
DaimlerChrysler	150 070
Royal Dutch/Shell Group	149 146
British Petroleum/Amoco	148 062
General Electric Co.	129 853
Mitsubishi Corporation	126 580
Toyota Motor Corporation	121 416

Source: Areport.com

CONCLUSION

Financial advisers in America have developed into high-revenue earners on the back of booming M&A and IPO markets. However, the cycle is currently moving the other way, and the firms are facing tough times ahead. They have had to announce lay-offs amounting to tens of thousands. The financial markets received a devastating blow on 11 September, and are only slowly recovering. One of the ways the major firms have sought to sustain revenues has been to broaden the range of products and services they provide, and as a direct consequence, many of the major institutions have become multi-disciplinary centres of financial excellence. Some financial services firms have had to cut down their presence in overseas markets, but as a general trend, they are continuing to extend their overseas reach to become truly financial multinationals, thereby empowering the ever-broadening globalization of financial services.

4

Raising of finance

OVERVIEW

One of the major tasks of the corporate financial adviser's work is to advise companies on the various types and sources of available finance. Their advice will depend on the purpose for which the finance is needed. They will need to formulate viable capital formation strategies and to create models that solve financial problems. Funds may be needed for the day-to-day trading operations of the company, for research/development, or for M&As/MBOs, MBIs, etc. In many acquisitions and MBOs, the main problem is to secure the necessary finance, and part of the financial adviser's brief is to secure financial support.

Raising equity finance is appealing, but may involve loss of control. But taking on debt finance may also be risky if there is uncertainty in the market. Whatever the option, a business plan will be required for presentation to fund-raising sources.

FUNDS FOR DAY-TO-DAY TRADING OPERATIONS

Bank overdraft

Many companies whether large or small, rely on banking overdrafts from their main bank or bankers. Overdrafts are available for bank customers exceeding their credit balance up to a limit subject to the bank's approval. Interest on the overdraft is charged on a daily basis, and can be fixed or variable.

Term loans

Term loans are repayable under a loan agreement through regular periodic payments, typically over periods of one to ten years, at fixed or variable interest rates. Fixed rate loans of up to 20 years are also available. Variable rates are typically 3 per cent above the bank's base rate. Loan rates are lower than overdraft rates.

Guarantee

A bank or other financial entity contractually undertakes to guarantee, or accept responsibility for the debt, default or failure of the company that has primary responsibility for the obligation. In other words, the guarantor is obligated in respect of the obligee of a third party (principal debtor or obligor) to pay the debt if the third party fails to perform. Guarantees are normally used to secure credit lines or raise credit for a specific purpose.

Structured finance

Structured finance is typically raised through finance providers other than the banks, including discount and factoring houses. Some banks also offer structured finance facilities, e.g., the HBOS. Structured finance lending is usually secured against company assets (securitization, asset-backed, mortgage-backed securities). The idea of using company assets grew out of invoice discounting and factoring, and is now used for a wide range of assets.

Structured finance is often used in MBOs and MBIs. Using structured business finance enables the new management team to retain control of the equity.

ASSET FINANCE

It is becoming increasingly common for companies to obtain asset finance through finance houses. This finance method is not a new idea. Some finance houses have been providing finance in this way for many years. There are two main ways of raising asset finance: through leasing or hire purchase. In leasing, the ownership of the asset remains with the finance provider. Leasing can be a finance or an operating lease, with different accounting and tax rules applying. With hire purchase, the asset may be acquired under an option at the end of the payment period. Hire purchase offers tax advantages, since tax deduction can be claimed.

The Finance and Leasing Association

The UK members of the Finance and Leasing Association provided £23.7 billion worth of business finance to the UK business sector in 2000, representing 25.7 per cent of all fixed capital investment in the UK. Martin Hall, Director General of the Finance & Leasing Association, said, 'The asset finance industry finances an array of equipment and other assets, from machine tools to heavy goods vehicles, from aircraft to computer systems. Our survey shows that asset finance is being used to finance investment in the British transport infrastructure, and IT sectors. It is helping small and medium-sized firms to increase their investment.'

LOANS FOR HIGH-VALUE ACQUISITIONS

- *Syndicated loans* are arranged by banks for high-profile borrowers requiring leveraged, project and acquisition-related finance (such as British Aerospace, British Telecom, DaimlerChrysler). Two or more banks act as security for the bulk of the loan, with one acting as the lead manager. The loans are also provided as working capital loans for financial institutions, and for emerging markets transactions.

- *Leveraged loans* are part of the syndicated loan segment and are used in high-value acquisitions or leveraged buy-outs. Such loans are bank loans of below investment grade issuers with floating interest rates typically based on LIBOR.

  The loans are often senior secured obligations at the top of the issuer's capital structure. Such loans are the most profitable of loans in corporate lending due to their secured nature. Leveraged loans or credit are often used in leveraged buy-outs where the assets of the firm guarantee the bulk of the loans taken out. Providers of leveraged loans receive fairly high fees, with the possibility of greater returns.

FUTURES AND OPTIONS

A more speculative way of raising funds is to deal in futures and options. Futures trading consists of the buying and selling of commodities, foreign exchange or securities under contracts providing for the delivery of specific amounts, at a particular price and at some specified future date, but physical delivery does not take place.

An option can be in the form of a contract between a bank and a customer, which gives the buyer the right (but not the obligation) to buy (call option) or sell (put option) a specified number of securities (usually 100 shares), currency units or commodities at a specified exercise (strike) price on a specified exercise day. In contrast to such non-tradable options, traded options (as the name implies) are actively traded on exchanges specializing in options and financial futures.

EQUITY CAPITAL

Equity capital is usually raised by start-ups or high growth companies needing capital for development purposes. The usual sources approached for such funding are:

- business angels
- incubators
- venture capitalists
- mezzanine finance
- private equity funding
- Private placing (placement)
- initial public offering on a recognized stock exchange (IPO)
- dual/multiple listing.

Business angels

Business angels are individuals or groups of individuals who support start-ups or entrepreneurs looking for seed capital to carry an idea or business proposition forward. A business angel may or may not seek active involvement in the new venture once it is up and running. However, to ensure that the proposition is viable, the business angel will usually look at budgets, projections and marketability from a professional angle. Since venture capital is not usually available in the UK for businesses with no track records, business angels are often the only source of finance for entrepreneurs with marketable ideas. The business angels are not organized into any one representative body, and may therefore be difficult to find. Advertising in financial papers is one way of getting in touch, another is through personal contacts.

Modus operandi

In recent years, companies and groups have been established in the UK to co-ordinate investor and business angel activities, and there are now some 30 formal entities in the UK. Proposals from entrepreneurs and companies are being considered on a formal basis, and in many cases, a small engagement fee is charged for the initial presentation. Matching of business angels with investors takes place through personal introductions, databases, circulation of proposals to members, 'investor fairs' and other means such as the internet. The biggest group in terms of investors, National Business Angels Network Ltd, has some 1600 investors on their books. Funding for individual deals varies. It can be as high as £500 000, but is normally in the range of £10 000 to £25 000.

Equity stake

Angels invest directly in private companies in return for an equity stake and may take a seat on the company's board. Tax incentives may be available if certain conditions are fulfilled under the Government's Enterprise Investment Scheme.

Incubators

In the US, a number of so-called incubators have been active for some years to provide capital for start-ups, but are now on the decline. They are accessible through the net. Incubators, as the name implies, nurse a company along, will encourage entrepreneurship, and will typically provide seed capital and offer technical and commercial assistance in the early phase. Incubators have especially targeted high-tech companies, providing funds, shared resources and intellectual capital.

Venture capitalists

Venture capital funds in the UK are normally raised by private companies that already have a track record. Venture capital is risk capital and the venture capital firms will typically take a stake in the equity and charge a high rate of interest on the capital injected. They are not usually in the company for the longer term and will therefore normally look for a profitable exit at the end of, say, a three-year period. UK venture capital firms are much more cautious than their US counterparts, and usually insist on a track record of two or three years before investing. Figure 4.1 illustrates the statistics for private-equity returns in the UK, the US and Europe.

Fig. 4.1 **Comparative private-equity returns in the UK, the US and Europe**

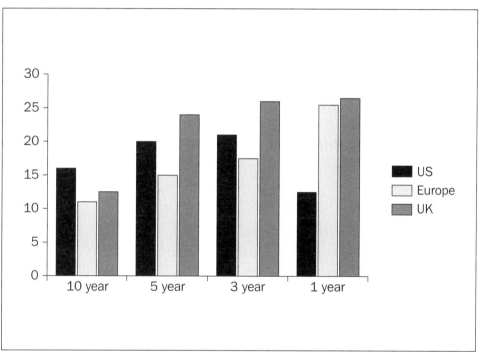

Source: London Business School, graph drawn up by BVCA, 31 December 1998.

Largest in Europe

The UK venture capital industry is the largest in Europe, with some 49 per cent of all venture capital investment (1999), and is second only to the US in the world. More than £35 billion has been invested through the venture capital industry in the UK between 1983 and 1999. In 2000, £6.3 billion was invested in UK companies, out of which £1.5 billion was put into high-tech companies. About 50 per cent of venture capital goes towards expansion.

Ways of investing

Venture capital is typically supplied to unquoted companies and involves the injection of capital in return for equity. Often, venture capital is supplied to technology-related companies with a high degree of risk. In this way, the venture capitalist becomes a part-owner of the business, and to ensure the return of his investment, has a strong interest in the success of the company.

Market slowdown

The venture capitalists are no longer competing fiercely for funding opportunities. With the attraction of lucrative returns on companies going public falling away, venture capitalists can afford to take more time to look at the propositions that are placed before them. From hardly having enough time to look at business plans and models, venture capitalists now take a long time to make up their minds. Due diligence is much more thorough. Venture capitalists are looking not only for ideas and new products, but also strong management teams with previous experience.

Whilst venture capitalist investment in new companies has slowed, it has not dried up completely. In the high-tech sector, venture capitalists focus on companies bringing saleable new software and hardware to the market, such as the development of special purpose chips.

Venture capital covers a wide range of situations, from start-ups through expansion, acquisitions and MBOs/MBIs.

Firming up a deal

Once a company has received an initial expression of interest from the venture capital company, possibly in the form of a letter of intent, heads of agreement or a subject to contract offer letter, the process of firming up a viable deal begins. As with flotations on the stock exchange, the venture capitalists will carry out their own due diligence on the company.

Follow-up appraisal

Whereas the initial appraisal is formed on the basis of a business plan and meetings with the company and individuals involved, a full investigation will be needed later on. This includes an examination of the company's history and track record to date, with details of founders and disclosure of financial performance. An in-depth review of the management team will focus on their background and special skills, and the particular expertise they bring to the company.

Product appraisal

The product appraisal will be thorough, with a description of the products and services, how the products work, who the clients are, and why the clients should prefer the company's products to others. Are there any unique features? What are the pricing policies, and how do prices compare with the competition. Is there any on-going research and development? Are any of the products produced under licence, or patented? Environmental, safety and health and regulatory issues will also be examined.

Marketing opportunities

The venture capitalist will closely examine the market opportunities for the company, and developments in the markets over a period of time. Points to be raised are the geographical size of the market, target customers and market influences. What is the company's market share at present, and what is it expected to be in the future?

The marketing and sales strategies of the company should be explained. Is there a sales force, and what area does it cover? Are the sales people on commission or salary, or a combination of both? What is the current order book position? Is there an advertising budget? How are products being marketed?

Future prospects

The company's strategies for the future should be set out in sufficient detail to provide a picture of how growth is going to be achieved. Bank references are also required; the venture capitalists are likely to bring in their own independent accountancy firm for an opinion on the accounts.

Financials

As always, the financials are of extreme importance to the providers of funds. The financial information should include audited accounts, usually for a period of three years, with summaries of the P&L account and balance sheet. Recent management accounts and budgets are also required, together with financial projections.

Once the venture capitalist is satisfied that the future prospects are viable, and there are no problems from the past, or indeed the present, final approval and an offer letter are likely to be forthcoming. The company may be required to sign warranties, which will be negotiated through lawyers. The venture capitalist may want a director on the board to monitor progress.

Mezzanine finance

Mezzanine finance is provided to firms seeking capital for expansion, acquisitions, MBOs, etc. It is usually in the form of loan capital and an equity stake. An example of a company specializing in providing mezzanine finance is the UK IFG Capital Ltd. They provide Mezzanine finance to small to medium-sized companies with a turnover of from £3 million to £50 million. Some companies, such as pure property, media and entertainment, as well as private individuals are excluded. The finance is available from a fund. IFG set up the Industrial Mezzanine Fund in 1997 with funds from institutions, banks, pension funds and investors, as well as having the backing of the European Investment Fund. Mezzanine finance is supplied as a subordinate loan, with an equity stake. Repayment is typically over five years at sums of up to £3 million per annum.

Private equity funding

The concept of private equity funding has taken hold in recent years. Private equity is taking over from venture capital, but venture capital is not the only source of private equity, which can also be generated from banks, government incentive schemes and private equity funds. Private equity is sought by SMEs and start-ups for early stage funding, expansion purposes and MBOs/MBIs. Deals are often done with companies below the mid-market size, and although they can be uneconomic, the thinking is that they are likely to lead to bigger future deals.

The accounting firms were among the first to enter the private equity market. Arthur Andersen, for instance, branched out into private equity in the 1990s. Recently investment banks have set up specialist private equity teams.

The British Venture Capitalist Association has released figures which show that private equity has grown into a financial sector in its own right, and in the UK concentrates on the mid-market. Deals can be anything from £50 million to £300 million. Figure 4.2 illustrates these statistics.

Fig. 4.2 Value of private equity invested annually in the UK funds

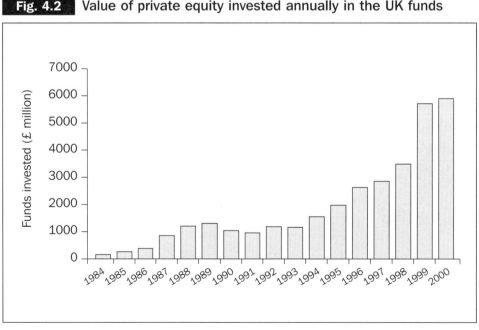

Source: BVCA, 2001

UK private equity industry is now recognized by institutional or investors as an asset class in its own right, and as a result, institutions are directing more funds towards UK private equity. UK private equity funds have generated attractive returns, and this has contributed towards a higher level of interest in this type of fund, not only in the UK, but also from US institutional investors and European investors.

Private placing

A private placing can be used by a private company to raise funds directly from investors, financial institutions and private individuals. It is often used as early stage financing. Shares may be sold without going through a stockbrokers or intermediaries. The placing may consist of new equity to be used for the paying off of expenses and debt incurred in connection with an acquisition or for new acquisitions.

Private placements in the US

In the US a private placing is called a private placement. A private placement memorandum is issued by the company doing the placement, stating the maximum offering of stock and the price per share. An offering period will be given (e.g., 30 days from a given date), with possibilities for an extension. Funds received from investors will be immediately available to the company. Unless the securities become publicly tradable through a registered broker/dealer and the filing of the appropriate forms with the authorities, the sale of the securities will be restricted, under an exemption (contained in No. 504 of Regulation D of the Securities Act of 1933), and may be sold to accredited or overseas investors (defined in the Act). If brokers/dealers are participating in the placement, a commission will be offered.

The net proceeds of an offering can also be used for general corporate purposes, including the implementation of marketing plans, new product research and development programmes, expansion of manufacturing capacity, and working capital.

Financial rewards for employees

Share option schemes

As part of the package for taking a company public, the corporate financial advisers will advise on how to set up share option schemes for employees. Such share option schemes, called share option plans in the United States, are instrumental in retaining key employees following a flotation or an M&A. Employees are given the right to sell a number of their shares at a stated price at some future time. If the shares go up in the meantime, employees can make a substantial gain. An important part of the financial adviser's role is to ensure that a company on flotation has the right top executives, and attracting such executives is becoming increasingly difficult in the absence of an attractive share option scheme.

Continued ...

Pension schemes

With the introduction of the Government's new stakeholder pension scheme, corporate financial advisers may also be called in to advise companies, especially SMEs who may not have an existing scheme. The new regulations require companies to introduce a pension scheme if they do not already have one in place; companies with less than five employees are exempt. The requirements for the new stakeholder pensions are enshrined in the Welfare Reform and Pensions Act 1999 and the Stakeholder Pension Schemes Regulations 2000.

Employee protection

Insurance

Financial advisers not only advise on how to raise finance, but also on how to protect their clients from unforeseen circumstances, such as the death of a key member of staff, usually the managing director or other key director. This is perhaps more relevant for small companies where the future of the company depends on one man. However, if a company's success depends on one man, with specialized knowledge for instance, the financial advisers will recommend that a key man insurance by taken out on flotation, and they will refer the client to appropriate insurance providers. For executives of large companies, key man insurance policies providing millions of pounds of cover are not unusual.

Other forms of insurance, such as professional liability insurance, will also be introduced by the financial advisers, if not already in place.

IPOs/flotations

The corporate financial advisers play a major role in advising companies seeking funds from primary and secondary markets. The flotation process is discussed in Chapter 5. Companies already floated on the stock market may go for dual or multiple listings to seek further capital in international markets. Dual listings may follow from the merger of two companies listed on two separate exchanges (e.g., BHP/Billiton). Multiple listings occur when major firms list on more than two exchanges.

Table 4.1 gives a schedule of new issues listings by the main market, AIM and Ofex.

Early stage financing

Private placings can also be raised to enable a company to go forward to an IPO. One example is the pre-IPO finance arranged by ARM Corporate Finance for a business developing software for educational purposes.

Table 4.1 Schedule of new issues listings: main market, AIM and Ofex, UK, December 2001 to Spring 2002

Name	Broker	Dealings start	Business	Size	Price	Type	Market	Raising
Stagecoach Theatre	Beeson Gregory 0207 488 4040	12-Dec	Drama School	£10m	93p	P&O	AIM	£4m
Telford Homes	Shore Capital 0207 408 4080	14-Dec	Housebuilder	£10m	50p	P	AIM	£4.4m
Expomedia	Charles Stanley 0207 739 8200	14-Dec	Exhibition Centres	£26m	75p	P	AIM	£3m
Pathway One VCT	Beaumont Cornish 0207 628 3396	17-Dec	Investment Company		25p	O	Ofex	£4.68m
DDD	Old Mutual 0207 489 4600	20-Dec	3D Software				AIM	
First Aid Corporation	Seymour Pierce 0207 648 8700	21-Dec	Sports management	£27m		P	AIM	£6m
Clean Diesel	Peel Hunt 0207 418 8900	end Dec	Pollution reduction	£13m		P	AIM	
Coinmaster	Daniel Stewart 0207 374 6789	end Dec	Fruit machines	£8.3m	55p	P	Ofex	
Wigmore Group	Seymour Pierce 0207 648 8700	2-Jan	Public sector repairs	£2.6m		P&O	AIM	
The Accessory People	Baker Tully 0207 413 5100	10-Jan	Mobile Accessory Wholesaler	£3.5m	n/a	listing only	Ofex	n/a
Matchroom Sport		Jan	Sports programming					
Croma	Peel Hunt 0207 418 8900	Jan	Surveillance equipment				AIM	
Doctors Direct	Loeb Aron 0207 628 1128	Jan	Emergency Doctors	£3m		O	Ofex	£1m
London & Boston Investments	Matrix Corporate Finance 0207 439 6050	Jan	Investment Company	£4m		P	Ofex to AIM	
BCD	Matrix Corporate Finance 0207 439 6050	Jan	Electronics engineering	£5m		listing only	Ofex	
BetOnSports	Seymour Pierce 0207 648 8700	Feb	Online betting	£100m		P	AIM	£25m
Flying Scotsman	Daniel Stewart 0207 374 6789	end Jan 2002	Steam Train	£2.5m	38p	O	Ofex	£2.2m
Ratners Online	Matrix Corporate Finance 020 7292 0825	early 2002	Online Jewellery	£9m		O	Ofex	£1.5m
Chapada Diamonds	SG Securities 0207 638 9000	early 2002	Diamond Mining	£30m		P	AIM	
Amersham Biosciences		Spring 2002		£2.4bn			Main	
Unicorn Aim VCT	Matrix Corporate Finance 0207 292 0825	2002	Investment Company	£35m		O	AIM	£35m
Quester VCT 5	Beeson Gregory 0207 488 4040	2002	Investment Company	£25m		O	Main	£25m
Photo Therapeutics	Investec Henderson Crosthwaite	2002	Medical Equipment	£50m		P	Main	£12.5m
Sense-Sonic	Gilbert Elliott 0207 369 0300	2002	Hearing Aids	£10m		P	AIM	

Source: *Investor's Week* (2002) Vol. 3, No. 1.

CONCLUSION

Advising clients on the raising of finance and on the optimal structuring of finance are major weapons in the financial advisers' armoury. The wrong structuring of finance can be a costly mistake. The financial advisers will recommend what proportion of debt and equity the company should aim for to finance its assets, and will recommend the best ways of achieving this. With the myriad of funding alternatives now available in financial markets, specialists are able to work out the right package of funding for their client. Reputable corporate financial advisers will help their clients avoid pitfalls in choosing ways of raising money. They will advise the client for instance, not to use short-term finance for long-term purchases such as machinery and equipment. The advisers will also point out the relative merits of buying, leasing or hiring of specific items. Apart from the more traditional ways of raising finance, such as bank loans, overdrafts and venture capital, the financial advisers will help their clients consider other ways of raising funds, such as structured finance, or in the case of small businesses, business grants, including the Government's Loan Guarantee Scheme. If large sums are required for expansion, a flotation may be the answer.

5

Listing on the stock exchange

REQUIREMENTS FOR LISTING

If clients wish to list on a stock exchange, the financial advisers will steer them through all the legal requirements and form filling. For listing on the stock exchange, the listing requirements have to be met. Whereas formerly the LSE was in charge of the listing requirements, this task has now been passed over the financial services authority. Some of the listing rules are mandatory under the legislation passed according to the EU stock exchange directives, and others are imposed by the FSA in its role as the competent authority. The FSA is now invested with powers to change the rules. The requirements that have to be satisfied for the FSA to approve a share issue for listing, broadly relate to the following:

- the persons responsible for the listing, the auditors and other advisers
- the shares for which application is made
- the issuer and its capital
- the group's activities
- the issuer's assets and liabilities, financial position and profits and losses
- the management
- the recent development and prospects of the group.

A set of requirements also relates to the persons responsible for the listing particulars, the auditors and other advisers.

METHODS OF LISTING

The financial advisers will advise the clients on the appropriate methods of listing of securities open to them, for securities already listed, i.e.:

- an offer for sale
- an offer for subscription
- a placing
- an intermediate offer
- a rights issue
- an open offer
- an acquisition or merger issue (or vendor consideration issue)
- a vendor consideration placing
- a capitalization issue (or bonus issue) in lieu of dividend or otherwise
- an issue for cash
- a conversion of securities of one class into securities of another class

- an exercise of options or warrants to subscribe securities, or

- such other method as may be accepted by the UK Listing Authority.

REASONS FOR LISTING

The reasons for listing can vary. The company may suffer from a shortage of capital for expansion. Existing shareholders and investors may be reluctant to put in sufficient funds. Or investors may want to seek an opportunity to realize their investment. The advisers will also point to the advantages of being able to trade shares in a liquid market. Share option schemes for employees may be an attractive proposition when it comes to retaining key employees. In general, it may also stand a private company in good stead to go public, since suppliers and clients are more likely to regard the company as reliable when it is subjected to the rigours of the listing process and the subsequent financial discipline.

There are so many factors to be considered before a flotation is decided upon, that a company considering such a route to fund-raising would do well to appoint financial advisers at an early stage. Apart from anything else, the financial advisers can help the company decide whether to list or not.

The decision to seek a listing may be taken at Board level before financial advisers are appointed. But the sooner the financial advisers are in place, the better. Apart from anything else, a flotation requires sponsors and the financial advisers are expected to be prepared to act as sponsors to the issue. The sponsors chosen for the flotation have to be on the approved list of the FSA. The list includes investment banks, corporate finance houses, investment firms and accountants. Corporate stockbrokers who may or may not be the same firm as the financial advisers, should also be appointed at an early stage. Also required are accountants, tax specialists and lawyers, as well as PR advisers.

The importance of choosing the right advice cannot be overestimated. Many advisers are now multidisciplinary, and can supply all the various aspects of advice under one roof. But there are arguments in favour of having separate advisers for each speciality, to avoid conflicts of interest, and many companies prefer to do this.

Once outside professional advisers have been selected, they will want to liaise with existing in-house advisers, such as accountants and solicitors.

In choosing advisers, some companies approach several different firms to discuss fees and expertise. It is also important to ensure that there is a meeting of minds. Most financial advisers require the submission of an outline proposal or business plan before agreeing to meet the client.

Once financial advisers have been appointed, they will become increasingly involved with the company, to such an extent that the company may feel the financial advisers are exercising too much influence in directing events. The financial advisers will even go so far as to look at the composition of the Board and recommend changes to or strengthening of the Board by advising on the appointment of new members before flotation.

The financial advisers may also take on the role of corporate brokers if they have such a facility within their organization. If not, they will be able to advise on a suitable broker, such as a broker specializing in a sector compatible with the company's product lines, e.g., biotechnology. The broker will not only place the shares from the flotation, but is likely to remain the future broker of the company once it is floated.

THE SPONSOR

A company seeking a listing is required to have a sponsor by the FSA, usually a corporate broker. The sponsor's primary function is to advise the company on the listing rules and how to comply with the various requirements, such as disclosure requirements. If a firm goes for a secondary listing, there are also rules to be observed. However, a firm can change its sponsor should they wish to do so. The sponsor must be on the FSA register of sponsors. A sponsor may or may not be the underwriter. An underwriter is not required by the FSA, and is purely a financial arrangement. The underwriter will guarantee that the issue is taken up.

Taking on a sponsorship is not a light-hearted affair, and just as company members will want to re-assure themselves that they have made the right choice, so the financial advisers will carry out stringent checks on the firm and its financial viability before they agree to take it on, unless the firm is already a large well-established company.

PHASES IN THE FLOTATION PROCESS

A company going for a flotation must be prepared for a lengthy process. In some cases, planning for the flotation starts one or even two years ahead of the event. But once the flotation process begins, the timetable is quite tight. Once the accountants' report on the company has been approved by the financial advisers, the period to flotation is typically 24 weeks. Financial advisers in the US maintain that they can float a company on Nasdaq in three months, but usually, this time scale is not achieved. In the UK, flotations have also known to have been completed in three months. The flotation proceeds roughly according to a schedule recommended by the London Stock Exchange and approved by the financial advisers.

The flotation process consists of three distinct phases.

12–24 weeks before listing

This pre-flotation stage is the period when the actual listing process begins. Corporate financial advisers are appointed, and engagement letters and instructions are sent out. The advisers will issue documents relating to the flotation and assess the market potential, and will ask for documents needed from the company. The professional advisers include the sponsors and brokers, and lawyers and accountants, if not already in place. Discussions are held between the Board and the advisers about the planned flotation. The structuring of the issue, including the percentage of shares to be issued to the public, will be discussed. A detailed timetable, usually drawn up by the lawyers, is drawn up and agreed upon. Work on the prospectus should already have been started. The reporting accountants begin their due diligence process.

6–12 weeks before listing

The first draft prospectus will be produced, and any problems areas, such as impending litigation, manufacturing bottlenecks, accounting backlogs, etc., will be reviewed. Other documentation will also be produced in draft form.

The important question of pricing the issue will be discussed. The UK Listing Authority will be approached for its reaction to the first draft documents, and there will be a meeting with the Stock Exchange to discuss the listing. The PR strategies will be discussed, and analysts briefed.

1–6 weeks before listing

During this period, further drafting meetings will be held, and a due diligence on the Prospectus will commence. The public relations people will start giving prominent publicity to the company, to make it known to investors. Road shows will present the company to investors. Road shows will involve members of the company, such as the managing director, the marketing director, etc. to explain the company's activities, prospects and future strategies. Submission of the formal documentation to the FSA will take place, and the first version of the Prospectus will be printed and distributed to the corporate advisers and company members.

One week before listing

- All documents to be in the hands of the FSA and approved by them
- Final pricing and allocation meeting to be held
- Registration of Prospectus
- Subscription agreement with the brokers to be signed

- Final Prospectus to be printed
- Admission week
- 48-hour documents to be submitted
- Formal application for listing and admission to trading to go forward
- Charges to be paid to the FSA and the stock exchange
- Permission to list and admission to trading to be granted
- Trading commences.

The timetable shown in Table 5.1 lists the various stages as well as the involvement of the various professional advisers in the respective processes.

Table 5.1 Flotation timetable

	Exchange	UKLA	Company	Sponsor	Accountants	Lawyers	PR
12–24 weeks before admission							
Appoint advisers			✓				
Detailed instructions to all advisers			✓	✓			
Detailed timetable list agreed	✓	✓		✓	✓	✓	
6–12 weeks before admission							
Review of problem areas			✓	✓		✓	
Draft Prospectus produced			✓	✓		✓	
Other documents in first draft				✓		✓	
Initial review of pricing issues			✓	✓			
First drafting meetings			✓	✓	✓	✓	
Draft documents submitted to FSA		✓		✓			
Initial meeting with the exchange	✓		✓	✓			
Review PR presentations							✓
Analyst presentation			✓	✓			✓
1–6 weeks before admission							
Drafting meetings			✓	✓	✓	✓	

	Exchange	UKLA	Company	Sponsor	Accountants	Lawyers	PR
Due diligence on prospectus			✓	✓	✓	✓	
PR meetings and road shows			✓	✓			✓
Formally submit and agree all documents and derogations with the FSA		✓		✓			
Bulk print preliminary Prospectus				✓		✓	
1 week before admission							
All documents completed and approved by FSA		✓	✓	✓	✓	✓	
Pricing and allocation meeting			✓	✓			
Allotment message sent		✓		✓			
Register Prospectus		✓		✓		✓	
Sign subscription agreement			✓	✓			
Bulk print final Prospectus				✓			
Admission week							
Submit 48-hour documents	✓	✓		✓			
Formal application for listing and admission to trading	✓	✓		✓			
Pay FSA and exchange charges			✓				
Listing and admission to trading granted	✓	✓					
Trading commences	✓						

Source: adapted from the London Stock Exchange promotional disc, Dec. 2000

Post-flotation

In the post-flotation stage, useful information is available from the register of shareholders, which can be used by the financial advisers, brokers and investor relations advisers to promote the shares. The share split between institutional and private investors, for instance, is revealed. Investor relations strategies, such as targeting a specific group of investors, and incentives to certain shareholders, can be formulated. The share register also gives warning of predators or other investors trying to build up a stake in the company

Flotation schedule summary

A useful summary version of the various stages in a flotation is provided by Deutsche Böerse's new schedule on the web (*see* Figure 5.1).

Fig. 5.1 Flotation schedule summary

Phase I Planning and preparation
- Selecting advisers and underwriting brokers
- Creating the legal requirements within the company
- Strategic discussion
- Preparing the schedule

Phase 2 Structuring
- Preparing the business and new issue concept
- Preparing the equity story
- Choosing the market segment
- Preparing the offering prospectus
- Due diligence
- Enterprise valuation
- Choosing the designated sponsor

Phase 3 Realization/marketing
- Briefing analysts
- Preparing research
- Publishing the offering prospectus
- Submitting the application for admission
- Targeting and contacting investors (e.g., road shows, IPO video chat, a multi-channel media contact between investors and company management)
- Preparing investor relations activities

Phase 4 Price determination
- i. Price determination and method of allocation
- ii. First trading day
- iii. Price stabilization and greenshoe option

Source: Deutsche-Böerse.com 2001

IPO test

The website also has an IPO test, which through a checklist gives companies an indication of whether they are ready to go public. The test assesses the company on ten points (*see* Table 5.2).

Table 5.2 IPO test

	Tick applicable column		
	Applies fully	Applies partially	Does not apply
1. The company already enjoys a favourable market position, and its growth potential ranges from good to excellent.			
2. The company is planning to raise additional equity capital to develop its competitive position.			
3. Pre-tax return on sales exceeds the sector average.			
4. The company has efficient accounting and controlling structures in place which incorporate subsidiaries and also allow regular reviews.			
5. First- and second-level management support the admission of additional shareholders and are prepared to submit to decision-making by new executive bodies if required.			
6. The company is prepared to create transparency for the capital market and to publish its up-to-date business on a regular basis.			
7. The company wants to enhance its profile in the media, to the public and to suppliers. At the same time, it wants to become an attractive choice for potential job applicants.			

	Yes	Planned	No
8. The company has the legal form of a publicly limited company or partnership limited by shares (or the relevant foreign equivalent) or is planning a conversion.			

	Less than 10%	5–10%	more than 10%
9. The return on sales exceeds 10 per cent and will also be maintained in future.			

	Tick applicable column		
	More than 3 years	1–3 years	Less than 1 year
10. The company which has been in existence for ... years, accounts for sales of approx. DM ... million (or currency equivalent) and is profitable.			

Evaluation: You have scored ... points out of a possible 10.

Source: Deutsche-Böerse.com 2001

Individual companies and their financial advisers can then use their scores to assess whether they are ready to go public.

WAYS OF ENTERING THE STOCK MARKET

The financial advisers may recommend one of three ways of raising capital from investors:

- *Initial public offer (IPO)*. In an IPO, the sponsor arranges for a percentage of the company's shares to be offered to investors, private or institutional at a fixed price. The sponsor will also arrange for underwriters who will agree to take up shares that are not sold during the flotation, against a fee.

- *Introduction*. The adviser may recommend that a company goes for an introduction, i.e., joining the stock market without raising capital. Through this method, costs are kept low, as there are no underwriting fees or costs for advertising. This method can be used if more than 25 per cent of shares are already in the hands of the public.

- *Placing*. In a placing, the company raises capital through offering its shares to selected institutional investors. With fewer shareholders, liquidity can suffer.

If the company is listing on the LSE, it is subject to the rules not only of the FSA, but also the LSE. The financial advisers will explain the different roles of the two entities. The FSA is legally responsible for reviewing and approving the Prospectus, which will be circulated to potential investors. The Prospectus is vetted by the financial advisers and gives information on the company and its activities, according to rules laid down by the FSA.

Most of the dialogue between the company and the FSA takes place through the financial advisers, although the company may come into direct contact with the FSA.

The responsibility of the exchange is to admit a company for listing. The LSE has its own admission and disclosure rules which are complementary to the FSA's rules. Both the LSE and the FSA have to approve the decision to proceed with the listing.

Once listed, a set of obligations and disclosure requirements has to be followed, such as sensitive information regarding the share price, and the timely release of annual financial results. In the US, companies listing on Nasdaq are required to report quarterly.

CHOICE OF STOCK MARKET

The financial advisers will advise a company on the factors affecting the choice of market to list on. A company may seek admission to a UK exchange, or an international exchange. If the company is already listed on a UK exchange, it may seek a duplicate or multiple listing elsewhere, to tap into larger capital markets.

In the UK, there are two significant markets.

The London Stock Exchange main market

The main market of the London Stock Exchange (LSE), also known as the Official List, is the principal market for listed companies from the UK and overseas. It has been operating since the 17th century, and lists some 2000 UK companies and 500 overseas companies. It provides companies with the means to raise capital through equity, debt and depository receipt issues and gives investors the opportunity to buy and sell shares in the companies of their choice.

Many companies like to list on the same Board as their peer groups. Listing on the LSE is regarded as highly prestigious and also helps to create a higher profile for the company, thus maintaining investor interest and awareness of their shares. But the main reason is usually to raise capital.

To list on the Official List of the LSE, a company has to be of a certain size, as it has to meet the UK Listing Authority's listing requirements, which stipulate that it must have a total capital of not less than £700 000.

Benefits of listing

The pros and cons of listing on the main market are identified by the financial advisers as follows.

- *Access to capital*. A listing on the main market provides access to equity capital not only on flotation, but also on a continuous basis through further capital raising as long as the company is quoted.

- *Providing a market for the shares.* The creation of a public market stimulates liquidity in the shares, which can be freely bought and sold. This may help to broaden the shareholder base, and provides an exit route for investors such as venture capitalists.

- *Greater acquisition opportunities.* New acquisitions can be made for shares or through the issuance of further shares.

- *Heightened public profile.* Through press attention and analysts' reports, the company is likely to become better known with the advantages this entails in terms of investor recognition, and greater customer awareness of the company's image, products and services.

- *Greater recognition from customers and suppliers.* The perception of the financial strength of a quoted company is much improved. This improved status may give the company access to better commercial and banking terms than would otherwise have been the case.

The list of benefits from listing supplied by the LSE is somewhat similar, but includes some additional points:

- *Broadened shareholder base.* This will give existing shareholders a chance to exit, should they wish to do so.

- *Objective market value placed on the company's business.* The financial advisers will ensure that independent valuation of the company takes place, to bring it to the market at the right valuation.

- *Employee commitment encouraged.* Share schemes, which the financial advisers can recommend, will encourage employees to achieve greater involvement and motivation.

- *Quoted shares have a specific market value.* They can be used in structuring acquisition deals, such as share swaps, or shares combined with cash.

- *Heightened company profile.* In turn, this increases the liquidity in the company's shares.

- *Enhanced status with customers and suppliers.* It is re-assuring for customers and suppliers to know that a company is listed on the stock market, which means that it has had to comply with a set of regulatory checks.

TechMARK

If the company is operating in the technology sector, it is advised to list on TechMARK. This division of the main market was set up in November 1999, and caters for the following areas of innovation and technology:

- computer hardware
- semiconductors
- telecommunication equipment
- computer services
- internet
- software.

A special streamlined application process is in place for companies belonging to the above sectors.

Table 5.3 TechMARK: best and worst in 2001

Best companies	Change over 1 year (%)	Losers	Change over 1 year (%)
Biotrace	373	Superscape	−90
Acambis	210	Netbenefit	−90
ITNet	92	Smartlogik	−90
Jasmin	88	Patsystems	−91
Theratase	50	Orchestream	−92
Synstar	47	Actrinic	−92
Total Systems	47	Horizon Technology	−93
Huntingdon Life	44	SR Pharma	−93
ICM Computer	39	Vocalis	−93
Druck	38	Colt Telecom	−93
Lynx	36	Zen Research	−94
iSoft	33	Marconi	−95
Xansa	32	Knowledge Support	−95
Smith & Nephew	30	Redbus	−95
KBC	23	Baltimore	−96
Eircom	23	Cedar	−96
Torex	22	Telecity	−98
Provalis	19	Bioglan	−98
Clinical Computing	17	Redstone	−98
Trace Computer	17	Scoot.Com	−98

Source: *Investor's Week* (2002) Vol. 3, No. 1.

AIM

Listing on AIM has the following major advantages:

- exposure to the UK market's liquidity
- respected regulatory standards
- unrivalled international expertise.

The main benefit of joining AIM is an opportunity for a company to raise funds for further growth. When listed on AIM, the company is in a public market which is specifically geared to raise funds.

AIM provides all the benefits of trading on a public market, but at the same time, it offers easier admission to the exchange, and a less stringent regulatory environment. Certain tax benefits are also in place.

Background

AIM was established in 1995 to attract growth companies from anywhere in the world and in 2001 had a total of some 850 companies listed, with 51 new companies joining that year, raising some £93 million. AIM-listed companies have a total market cap of £13.3 billion with individual market caps ranging from £2 million to more than £700 million. Companies attracted to AIM include young, venture-capital-backed businesses, as well as established family concerns. They represent a wide range of activities, from technology to distribution, restaurants and leisure. Newcomers include Proactive Spots, raising £13 million, and GW Pharmaceuticals, raising £25 million. AIM now also trades global depository receipts (GDRs), certificates representing a number of shares in a quoted company which allows investors to purchase shares in foreign companies in their home market. This allows the issuing company to raise capital in many markets.

AIM also attracts international companies (*see* Table 5.4).

Table 5.4 International companies: listing on AIM

Country	Percentage
Australia	17
Bermuda	14
Belize	3
Canada	8
Republic of Ireland	19
Israel	6

Country	Percentage
British Virgin Islands	6
Sweden	3
Netherlands	3
US	21
	100

Source: LSE, Statistics (2001) December

Table 5.5 Top 20 AIM companies by market capitalization

Company		Business sub-sector	Market capitalization £m
1	Peel Holdings	862	Real estate holding and development	758.20
2	SportingBet	532	Gaming	251.92
3	Intechnology	972	Computer services	231.32
4	Minorplanet Systems	596	Rail, road and freight	218.19
5	Aquarius Platinum Limited	48	Other mineral extractors and mines	209.80
6	Transense Technologies	313	Auto parts	198.34
7	Enterprise	581	Business support services	179.90
8	Ask Central	539	Restaurants, pubs and breweries	175.63
9	Tribal Group	583	Education, business training and employment agencies	143.69
10	Sibir Energy	73	Oil and gas – exploration and production	140.18
11	Patientline	673	Fixed-line telecommunication services	137.79
12	Chorion	538	Leisure facilities	135.81
13	Science Systems	977	Software	130.96
14	Carlisle Holdings Ltd	581	Business support services	115.81
15	Virt-X	879	Other financial	114.50
16	Big Yellow Group	581	Business support services	111.15
17	London Securities	588	Security and alarm services	110.09
18	International Greetings	460	Packaging	109.35
19	Tenon Group	879	Other financial	107.69
20	GW Pharmaceuticals	480	Pharmaceuticals	104.43

Source: LSE, Statistics (2001) December

The AIM listed companies are distributed by equity market value (*see* Table 5.6).

Table 5.6 Distribution of companies by equity market value

Market value range (£m)	AIM (UK & International)			
	No. of companies	%	Equity market value (£m)	%
Over 1000	0	0.0	–	0.0
500–1000	1	0.2	758.2	6.5
250–500	1	0.2	251.9	2.2
100–250	20	3.2	2 882.3	24.8
50–100	25	4.0	1 674.5	14.4
25–50	66	10.5	2 305.0	19.9
10–25	139	22.1	2 205.8	19.0
5–10	133	21.2	967.3	8.3
2–5	135	21.5	448.8	3.9
0–2	97	15.4	113.5	1.0
Unvalued securities	0	0.0	–	–
Suspended	11	1.8	–	–
Totals*	628	100.0	11 607.2	100.0
More than £50 million	47	7.5	5 566.9	48.0
Less than £50 million	570	90.8	6 040.3	52.0
Less than £25 million	504	80.3	3 735.3	32.2

* Excluding fixed interest securities

Source: LSE, Statistics (2001) December

Ofex

Ofex is an off-exchange facility provided by J.P. Jenkins Ltd for share trading. It is unregulated, but share information is published daily in the *Financial Times*.

Benchmark funds

Various fund managers have launched investment products using the FTSE Benchmark indices as performance benchmarks. Technology-based funds include the Close FTSE Benchmark fund (1999), a unit trust consisting of benchmark companies, the Invesco TechMARK Enterprise Trust which uses the FTSE

TechMARK 100 index as a benchmark, the Edinburgh Technology Fund, and the UK Techtornado Fund (Gartmore).

International exchanges

Many companies listed on minor domestic exchanges have turned to the international market and sought listing on exchanges in markets other than their own, such as the LSE and the main US exchanges. In the US, many international companies have listed on NYSE and Nasdaq as well as, or instead of on their local exchanges. Listing on NYSE is regarded as being very prestigious, and some companies from emerging countries list for this very reason, quite apart from the much greater liquidity and share turnover in the American markets. However, fees and costs of maintaining a presence are high, and should be weighed against the benefits.

The role of the financial advisers in undertaking dual listings is not dissimilar to the initial flotation, but it is rare for companies to use their local financial advisers, unless the advisers already have an international presence. Overseas companies listing on Nasdaq for instance are advised to appoint US corporate advisers who know their way around the financial markets, and who know the requirements of the SEC, including how to present the information required such as US-GAAP financial accounts, etc.

The recent IPO scope of activity on the American stock markets is illustrated by the figures shown in Table 5.7. Although the figures are not directly comparable, the considerable drop in activity on Nasdaq is apparent.

Table 5.7 IPO activity on Nasdaq, NYSE and Amex

	Nasdaq offerings	Dollar value of Nasdaq offerings (millions)	NYSE offerings	Dollar value of NYSE offerings (millions)	Amex offerings	Dollar value of Amex offerings (millions)	Total offerings	Total dollar value of offerings (millions)[1]
2000	397	$52 585.09	48	$59 699.95	6	$229.58	451	$112 514.62
Year to 2001	63	$7,840.04	35	$36,393.41	3	$26.00	101	$44,258.95

1. Dollar value of offerings include overallotment (if applicable)

Source: Nasdaq.com, January 2002

ENTERING THE MARKET VIA A SHELL COMPANY

Another way of entering the market, especially the OTC market in the US, is by reversing into a shell that is already quoted. The shell company has already been through the entire listing process, and the acquiring company, by reversing into it, therefore enters through the back door, so to speak.

A shell company should not be confused with a newly formed off-the-shelf limited liability private company. A UK off-the-shelf company has been formed and registered with Companies House, but has not yet traded. It is a clean, dormant company with a standard set of Articles of Association, usually formed by company formation agents to enable them to have ready-made companies available for immediate purchase off the shelf. Through a name change administered through the filing of a simple form, and if required, a change of the main objects clause in the Memorandum and Articles of Association, a company with a selected name (provided this is available) can then be set up speedily and at low cost.

The use of shells is widely practised in the US. For a private company to go in for an IPO is expensive and time-consuming. It takes several months to prepare for an IPO, and if market conditions turn out to be unfavourable, the IPO can be withdrawn on the advice of the financial advisers, thus causing more delays and costs. A 'reverse merger' through the acquisition of an already quoted company registered with the SEC, and up-to-date with its filings, therefore makes sense. Through the merger, the private company takes a majority stake. The change of ownership can be effected through a share swap, and through the issue of new shares. The existing Board then resigns, and a new Board consisting of the new owners is appointed. Through changing the name of the public company to that of the private company, the private company then becomes a public company. This whole process can be completed in a matter of weeks.

Rather than raising money through an IPO, the new public company can now trade its stock publicly and raise additional capital; or the shares, which now have a quoted value, can be used to acquire further companies.

Shell companies in the US, which typically have 50 million shares authorized, and perhaps 5 million shares issued, are for sale for anything between US$ 150 000 and US$ 300 000. However, the acquiring company must re-assure itself through proper due diligence that the publicly traded company is 'clean', i.e, that it has no undeclared liabilities or other problems pending, such as lawsuits or intransigent shareholders. One of the financial advisers' primary functions is to advise on the listing rules and to establish that the shell company is in good standing with the regulatory authorities. In some cases, companies are set up for the specific purpose of being used as vehicle for reversing into, and will therefore have no assets or liabilities, or operating history.

CONCLUSION

For listing on the stock exchange, the financial advisers come into their own. They will guide their clients through the intricate process of deciding on the best market for the company's shares in terms of liquidity and size, and in terms of the amount of capital the company can be expected to raise. For companies already listed, the financial advisers may be called in to help prepare for a dual listing. This may be a simpler process, depending on the requirements of the exchange selected. On the other hand, there may be hurdles such as differing accounting standards and regulatory regimes. Once a stock exchange has been selected, the financial advisers will assist the company in becoming accepted for listing through a series of steps involving *inter alia* the preparation of a Prospectus, the streamlining of the company's future capital structure, and the exhaustive due diligence process. The financial advisers, after sounding out the market, and taking into account prevailing economic conditions, will also advise on the price of the issue. Once the flotation has gone ahead, the financial advisers will typically maintain contact with the company, ensuring that reporting procedures are adhered to, that investor interest remains high, and that liquidity in the shares is maintained at a high level.

6

Private and public fund-raising – documents and processes

OVERVIEW

This chapter discusses the various documents required and processes applied in private and public fund raising.

THE BUSINESS PLAN

The initial step in capital-raising whether in a public or private market, is the preparation and submission of a business plan to interested fund-raising parties. This can be prepared by the company itself, or with the advice and even drafting of the corporate financial advisers. The priority given to a proper business plan is also reflected in the fact that in the United States a whole new industry of business plan consultants has sprung up. Their fees are usually US$ 10 000 upwards, or US$ 100+ per hour charged on a time-basis.

The importance of the business plan cannot be overstated. The business plan can make all the difference as to whether a company is accepted for flotation or for other fund-raising such as a private placing. A checklist for a typical business plan appears in Figure 6.1, and shows the various areas of information required.

Fig. 6.1 Business plan checklist

```
1. Executive summary ...................................................................

2. The industry .........................................................................
        Market segments .............................................................
        Demographics .................................................................
        Government regulations.....................................................

3. The company .........................................................................
        Business model ...............................................................
        Products and services .......................................................
        Strategic alliances ..........................................................
        Management information systems ..........................................
        Human resources .............................................................
        Purchasing.....................................................................
        Insurance......................................................................
        Legal ...........................................................................
        Operations – current and development period ...........................
        Business locations ...........................................................
```

Continued ...

Fig. 6.1 Continued

4. Marketing strategy ....
- Competition/competitive approach ....
- Marketing strategy and promotion ....

5. Management ....
- Executive officers ....
- Board of directors ....
- Management board ....
- Finance committee ....
- Other committees ....

6. Risk factors ....

7. Transactions summaries ....
- Investor transaction ....
- Use of proceeds ....

8. Projected financial statements ....
- Basis for projected financial statements ....
- Revenue ....
- Staffing/payroll ....
- Other general and administrative expenses ....
- Miscellaneous notes ....
- Projected income statement, five years ....
- Projected balance sheet, five years ....
- Projected cash flow, five years ....
- Projected revenue schedule, one year ....
- Detailed revenue projections ....
- Staffing schedule, one year ....
- Payroll schedule, one year ....

Confidentiality agreement

The business plan is normally preceded by a non-disclosure or confidentiality agreement. This agreement signed by the parties concerned constitutes a guarantee that confidential information supplied by the parties to the agreement should not be disclosed to any third party, except with the consent of the parties to the agreement.

Short version business plans

The business plan can be a lengthy document, but in recent years, a shorter form has emerged, particularly in the case of start-up IT companies that do not necessarily have a long history or track record. One of the reasons for the short form business plan is that financial advisers simply do not have the time to read lengthy business plans, and may decide whether to go for a project on the basis of a condensed plan with all the relevant facts.

Contents

There is no hard and fast rule as to the contents of a business plan, but over the years, a format has involved which essentially contains the following elements.

- *Executive summary.* An important section of the business plan is the executive summary, which should set out in clear language what the activities and future objectives of the company are, and what is hoped to be achieved through the fund-raising.

- *The industry section.* This section gives an overview of the industrial sector in which the company operates, in terms of its structure, market segments and local/international demographic factors. Government regulations specific to the industry may also be included if such regulations materially affect the location of the business, its operations and marketing potential.

- *The company section.* The company section gives a comprehensive overview of the company, its management, products and services, and operations. The company's business model may be expressed in an organization chart showing the structure of the firm in terms of functions such as sales, production, IT, human resources, etc. A traditional chart will show the chain of command, lines of responsibility and spans of control. The structure may also contain the names of senior executives in charge of departments or divisions. A geographical chart will show the various locations of the company either locally or on an international basis, or both.

  The products and services offered by the company will be outlined. If the reason for the offering is to develop or market new products, these will be described in depth.

  The company may have strategic alliances in its field, which may add strength to the range of products and services it is able to offer, or to its marketing reach. The nature and scope of the alliances if any, will be discussed.

  Other aspects such as purchasing, insurance and legal matters can also be brought into the company section, as well as property and legal matters.

- *Management information systems*. The company may wish to highlight and discuss factors such as its management information systems, IT infrastructure and internet capability.

- *Human resources* are a key determinant of a company's success, and adequate space should be given to a description of the work force. A separate section should be devoted to top personnel such as directors, managers, etc.

- *Operations*. The operations should be discussed in terms of current operations and development periods for new products.

- *Business locations*. The business locations should be listed, with a distinction between headquarters, manufacturing and R&D operations and sales operations, and any other relevant activities.

- *Marketing strategy*. This section should contain an analysis of the competition, with the names and size of competitors, markets affected and market share. Questions such as whether the competition relates to existing or new products, should be answered. The level of competitive risk should be assessed. The proposed marketing strategy should be clearly focused in terms of objectives, and should outline ways in which competition will be countered and minimized as well as the media proposed for promotion and advertising.

- *Risk factors*. The risk factors section of a business plan make for chilling reading. Although nothing is expected to go wrong, this section of the business plan does not express optimism. The risk factors section has expanded over the years, especially in the United States with its high penchant for litigation. Everything that can be guarded against is incorporated in the risk factors, to ensure full openness and to make sure the company cannot be accused of misleading investors, or lulling them into a false sense of security.

  The risks that may occur, are examined from every angle: financial, commercial and economic conditions, competition (any existing competition, new products entering the market), dependence on key personnel, growth factors, technology obsolescence, the cost of IT and other highly skilled and educated staff, no assurance of product success, and exchange risks. Operating expenses may increase more rapidly than revenue; insurance companies may refuse to insure against product risk. If the company relies on a particular group (e.g., doctors) for its marketing success and the group fails to respond, sales may suffer. Examples of clauses encompassing the above are:

  – Uncertainty of conditions in the market. There is no certainty that the (name of company) concept will be a profitable format. There is no certainty that the Company will be able to adapt its format to changing market conditions. There is no certainty that the Company will be able to operate as a successful format although the management believes that the flexibility within the format reduces its risk as the format will adapt to changing conditions.

– Dependence on key management personnel. The performance of the Company is dependent upon the active participation of personnel employed by the Company. Accordingly, no person should purchase shares unless he or she is willing to entrust all aspects of the Company's business to its management. Potential investors must carefully evaluate the personal experience and business performance of the principals of the Company. The loss of any of these key personnel could have an adverse effect upon the Company's ability to continue its business. Moreover, the ability and availability of management personnel to continuously function with regard to the Company's affairs may be adversely affected by, among other things, health problems, financial or personal difficulties, or responsibilities relating to other professional or other activities which could result in potential conflicts of interest between certain members of management and the Company.

– Working capital requirements: need for additional financing. The Company will require additional capital or other financing after the completion of this offering to finance its operations and continued growth. There can be no assurance that the Company will be able to obtain such financing if and when needed, or that if obtained, it will be sufficient or on terms and conditions acceptable to the Company. If the board of directors of the Company determines to obtain additional capital through the issuance of additional equity securities of the Company, there can be no assurance that such shares will be issued at prices or on terms equal to the offering price and terms of this offering. Any such future equity financing could be dilutive to holders of the Shares offered hereby.

– General economic and other conditions. The Company's business may be adversely affected from time to time by such matters as changes in economic, industrial and international conditions, changes in taxes, changes in government regulations, prices and costs and other factors of a general nature and in particular those changes which have an adverse material effect on the information technology sector or other industrial sectors in which the Company becomes engaged.

– Other risks. There is no guarantee that the present types or amounts of insurance coverage will be sufficient to protect the Company in the event of injury, accident, damage or liability arising out of the operation of the Company's resources.

- *Transaction summaries*. Disclosure of transactions between the issuers and other inside parties, which might seriously affect the future potential of the company.

- *Financial statements*. The financial statements may be limited to projections at the early stage of a business plan. In this context it should be noted that Projections are less binding on a company than forecasts. Projected income statements, balance sheets and cash flows are usually for a five-year period.

The financials are extremely important, and many investors turn to this section before reading anything else.

THE PROSPECTUS

The Prospectus is a written document required for listing and other securities offerings. The contents of the business plan, as modified, will form part of the Prospectus, which contains all the information required by the listing authority. It is a legal document providing written proof of relevant facts. As such, it protects the issuers and the brokers. The document is also used to sell the issue by the company itself and its broker/dealers. Investors will be given a copy of the Prospectus to help them decide whether or not to invest.

The information contained in the Prospectus provides a basis for comparison and assessment, with the most important information about capital structure, number and price of shares, etc. on the front page. The front page (or pages in the case of a large issue) contains all the material facts. It sets out the issuer's name, the financial and other advisers and the amount and class of securities offered. For these reasons, this page is very important. Busy investment firms often decide whether or not to invest in an issue purely from glancing at the names of the professional advisers on the front page.

Listing particulars

In the UK the prospectus is often referred to as the 'Listing particulars'. It is prepared by the company and its financial advisers, and contains all the information which has to be made public according to the UKLA's listing rules to enable them to make a decision about the offering. If a company is aiming for a placing or an IPO, a 'pathfinder' prospectus, also referred to as a 'red herring', may be issued. This is almost the same document as the Prospectus, except for the listing price. The pathfinder may be used to market the issue on a restricted basis.

Details of professional advisers

As an example, the Listing particulars for the introduction to the Official List of HBOS plc in connection with the merger of the Bank of Scotland and Halifax Group plc listed the professional advisers shown in Figure 6.2.

Fig. 6.2 Details of professional advisers in Listing Particulars of HBOS plc

Sponsor:	Cazenove
Registrar:	Computershare Investor Services Plc
AD Depository:	Morgan Guaranty Trust Co.
Auditors and Reporting Accountants:	KPMG Audit Plc
Halifax Group Plc/Bank of Scotland	Financial Advisers:
	Lazard
	Cazenove
	Gleacher & Co. Ltd
	Credit Suisse First Boston
	Dresdner Kleinwort Wasserstein
Legal Advisers as to English Law:	Linklaters
	Herbert Smith
Legal Advisers as to Scottish Law:	Maclay, Murray & Speas
	Tods Murray WS
Stockbrokers:	Merrill Lynch International
	Cazenove

Source: HBOS Listing Particulars, 2001

The EU – proposal for a new 'single passport' Prospectus

The EU Commission's proposal for a new 'single passport' Prospectus is discussed in Chapter 8.

The United States

Prospectuses submitted in the US have to conform to the strict requirements of the Securities and Exchange Commission (SEC). The SEC requirements are laid down in special forms to be submitted together with the application for listing, and are reflected in the Prospectus. The following is an example of the front page of a Prospectus for an IPO on Nasdaq.

Fig. 6.3 Front page of a Prospectus for an IPO on Nasdaq

Prospectus

4,000,000 shares

Name of company (company 'X')

Common Stock

This is Company 'X''s initial public offering of common stock. All the shares of common stock are being sold by company 'X'.

Prior to this offering, no public market existed for those shares. Our common stock has been approved for listing on the Nasdaq National Market under the symbol 'XXX'.

Investing in our common stock involves risks which are described in the 'risk factors' section beginning on page ___ of this Prospectus.

	Per share	Total
Public offering price.........................	$	$
Underwriting discount	$	$
Proceeds, before expenses, to company 'X'	$	$

The underwriters may also purchase up to an additional _____ shares of common stock from us at the public offering price, less the underwriting discount, within thirty days from the date of this Prospectus to cover over-allotments.

Neither the Securities and Exchange Commission nor any state securities commission has approved or disapproved these securities or determined if this Prospectus is truthful and complete. Any representation to the contrary is a criminal offence.

These shares of common stock will be ready for delivery on or about (date ___)

(e.g. **Merrill Lynch**

J.P. Morgan & Co.)

The date of this Prospectus is _____

Prospectus contents

The contents of a Prospectus will typically be as follows:

- summary of the Prospectus
- risk factors
- use of proceeds
- dividend policy
- capitalization
- dilution
- selected financial data
- management's discussion and analysis of financial condition and results of operations
- management
- transactions with directors, executive officers and ___ per cent stockholders
- principal stockholders
- description of capital stock
- shares eligible for future sale
- underwriting
- legal matters
- experts
- where to find more information
- financial statements.

PRIVATE PLACEMENT MEMORANDUM

Shares for private placement may be offered in a Private Placement Memorandum. An example of the front page of such a document for a US private placement is shown in Figure 6.4.

CONCLUSION

Fund-raising by financial advisers does not normally take place without documentation such as a business plan or a prospectus, or a private placement memorandum to present to investors. The business plan may be prepared by the company itself, or in consultation with the financial advisers. In the US, business plan consultants may do the work, under the supervision of the company or the financial advisers. The Prospectus contains standard information to provide a basis for comparison and assessment, with the most important information about capital structure, number and price of shares, etc. on the front page. A Prospectus underwritten by top financial advisers is likely to get a smooth ride past the listing authorities and to result in successful placement of the issue with the institutions and other investors.

Fig. 6.4 Front page of a US private placement memorandum

Confidential Private Placement Memorandum

Dated: _____

MAXIMUM OFFERING: 1,000,000 Shares at $1.00

Name of company (the 'Company') hereby offers to qualified purchasers as defined herein, for investment purposes, a maximum of 1,000,000 Shares of common stock at $1.00. (Sections on 'Description of securities' and 'Terms of the Offering' are included in the main body of the text.)

The Shares are offered by the Company (name and address of company). The Shares will be sold for an offering period of thirty days from (date), the date of this confidential Private Placement Memorandum (the 'Memorandum') expiring on (date). At the discretion of the Company the offering may be extended for an additional month until (date). There is no escrow account and no minimum number of Shares, which must be sold in the offering. Consequently all funds received from prospective investors will be immediately available to the Company for its use in accordance with the information contained in the memorandum. (Reference is made to 'Introduction and Summary', 'Terms of the Offering', 'Description of Securities' and 'Risk Factors'.)

While the Company intends that its securities may become publicly tradable through the filing of appropriate informational forms by an NASD registered broker dealer acting as a market maker, there is no guarantee that such a filing will take place. In the absence of such a filing, the Company's securities will be restricted. The Shares are offered without registration under state or federal securities laws, and have not been registered in accordance with the Securities Act of 1933, as amended (the '1933 Act') but are offered pursuant to an exemption contained in Rule 504 of Regulation D of the 1933 Act. Unless trading commences in accordance with appropriate federal rules and regulations, or unless subsequently registered, the Shares shall constitute an aliquot Investment, as unregistered, restricted securities. (See 'Risk Factors' and 'Description of Securities.')

Units are offered only to Investors qualifying as 'Accredited or Overseas Investors' as defined under Rule 50 1(a) of the 1933 Act. (See 'Exemption from Registration' and 'Eligibility Standards'.)

Continued ...

Fig. 6.4 Continued

Each unit consists of one (1) share of common stock. $.001 par value.

The Company reserves the right to name certain brokers/dealers to participate in the placement of the securities offered in this memorandum. If the Company places all the units, no commission will be paid.

	Price to the Public	Underwriting Commission	Net Proceeds to Company
Per unit	$1.00	$0.00	$1.00
Total Proceeds	$1,000,000.00	$0.00	$1,000,000.00

Name and address of company

The date of this Memorandum is _____

Transactional activities – the M&A market

OVERVIEW

The overriding objective of financial advisers appointed to assist in mergers and acquisitions is to maximize the return on the deals they are involved in, both in the immediate and the longer term, and to obtain the best possible price for their clients within a reasonable timeframe. To this end, the advisers follow the deals through right from the initial stages to the post-acquisition period. They apply their considerable expertise in identifying and evaluating targets, structuring and setting up the deals, assisting in negotiating the entire process, and helping the company through the post-acquisition integration phase. They ensure that as far as possible all risk factors are guarded against, and that accountancy, tax and regulatory issues are dealt with. They find as much relevant information as possible for their clients, all with the least possible disruption to their clients' business.

An important function of the financial advisers in some deals is to act as a go-between. They will target appropriate deals for an anonymous client, and start negotiations. This ensures the confidentiality of the client who may not wish to make it known that he/she is in the market as a buyer or a seller.

With uncertainty in the marketplace, M&A activity has plateaued, and deals are less frequent. But the driving forces behind deals still hold good. Growth prospects are still very much in the forefront of reasons for companies seeking deals. Through consolidation, economies of scale are likely to result. One industry that is reported to seek M&A consolidation as the answer to future price stability, is the mining industry which in its fragmented state is suffering from falling prices of metals and industrial minerals.

Companies used to seek rapid completion of deals, since hesitation or protracted negotiations could result in loss of market share. However, with recessionary trends, deal activity is slowing down. Some deals remain faster to complete than others. Deals involving companies from the same sector, for instance, tend to be less complicated and therefore faster since the due diligence process is easier and less protracted than in the case of companies seeking targets with different products or at different stages in the value chain.

Spin-offs

Whilst M&A activity may be slowing down, divestitures or the spinning off of business unit from existing companies are becoming big business for the financial advisers. Spin-offs may occur where restructuring is necessary, for instance, to raise cash for companies in default.

DRIVERS OF M&As

M&As can be used as a way for companies seeking a flotation to gain scale. Some public companies are looking to acquire private companies for this purpose, or in the hope that their access to capital markets will improve. However, this does not always work, since the gain in profitability may not be commensurate with the size of the deal, and margins may suffer.

Depressed share values may create opportunities for acquisitions. However, today's markets are primarily seeking increased revenue and a sustained rise in profitability. Proven synergies are an added advantage.

M&A in banking institutions

More light was thrown on the drivers of M&A in a study published by the European Central Bank in December 2000 on mergers and acquisitions in the EU Banking industry. M&As in the banking sector are not, in the opinion of the ECB, the driving forces of change in themselves, but are made in response to changes in other sectors, such as information technology, the integration of international capital markets, and with particular relevance to Europe, the introduction of the euro. Recent mergers in the banking sector are not solely among the banks themselves, but are often alliances between banking organizations, telecommunications, software and internet companies.

In the late 1980s and early 1990s, M&As were part of the restructuring and concentration process which took place within the smaller countries. The large national institutions that resulted were better equipped to compete in international markets. The majority of M&As was in the domestic area (80 per cent). M&As also took the banks into emerging markets, particularly in countries with historical ties, such as Spain and Portugal expanding into Latin America.

The data collected showed that domestic bank M&As were usually in the form of mergers, with differences between EU member states. Mergers outnumbered acquisitions in Austria and Germany. In France and Italy, the opposite was the case.

INFORMATION REQUIRED FOR THE M&A PROCESS

M&A is a complex process. The information required for the merger/acquisition of a company is not unlike what is required for a flotation on the stock market, and presents as complete a picture as possible of the company and its prospects. The financial advisers will ensure that the information needed is up-to-date. Typically, the following areas will be covered:

- an up-to-date business plan
- Product information sheets
- Product and sales literature, PR material
- Market analysis: competitors, prospects
- Organization chart
- Information on employees, shareholders, directors
- Up-to-date financials – cash flows, balance sheets, P&L statements, forecasts
- Budgets
- Tax liabilities
- Litigation, past, present, pending
- Real estate (ownership, leases)
- Intellectual property.

THE DEAL PROCESS

The steps in a typical M&A deal process are summarized by Pricewaterhouse-Coopers. Their transaction services assist clients in acquisitions, divestitures and strategic alliances, as well as access to global markets in general. The various stages in a deal are:

- *Strategic deal planning*
  - No-access due diligence
  - Bid support
  - Vendor assistance
- *Deal execution*
  - Sell-side due diligence
  - Market due diligence
  - Financial and tax due diligence
  - Deal structuring
  - Global capital markets
  - Operational improvement
- *Harvesting deals*
  - Post-deal services
  - The accelerated transition
  - M&A risk services.

Strategic deal planning

No-access due diligence may be needed in hostile takeovers, or in takeovers of foreign companies where access to information is denied or difficult. Bid support can take the form of a defensive 'dummy' run for companies who are fearing a takeover. As part of the defence, areas of vulnerability within the target are identified. Possible 'white knights' to assist against hostile bidders may be identified. Poison pills may be part of the targeted company's defence. Assistance is given to vendors wanting to sell their business, to ensure they obtain the best possible price.

Deal execution

The seller can commission an independent due diligence report on his company. Financial advisers will undertake legal responsibility for the report *vis-à-vis* potential purchasers. If accepted by the buyer, this may speed up the process. A sell-side due diligence also limits interruption of the day-to-day management process, and may increase the value achieved for the business, since problems and other deal issues can be ironed out by the seller in advance, rather than during the negotiation process. This avoids problem areas being used by the buyer as negotiation points.

The due diligence process is important since it guards against surprises which might scupper the deal. It is the aim of the due diligence process to examine all possible outcomes.

Financial advisers also offer invaluable assistance in spin-offs or carve-outs from existing businesses. Such deals can be very complex, and require adequate forward planning of the separation process to avoid disruptions and loss of revenue.

To evaluate forecasts and projections from a target company, it is important to draw parallels with other competitors in the industry sector. Financial advisers have analysts specializing in the various sectors, who will be able to provide a market due diligence for a relevant sector. This will enable the purchaser to assess whether the target company has put forward a realistic picture of its future earnings potential.

Key areas such as financial performance and tax issues are scrutinized by the financial advisers, to ensure that the acquisition target is indeed a viable proposition and that the valuation of the company as reflected in the price is realistic.

The financial advisers will structure deals to optimize the interests of their client shareholders, directors and other beneficiaries within the art of the possible in terms of taxation, regulatory issues and commercial realities, as well as the finance available. Special solutions are available for brick and mortar companies wanting to acquire e-businesses.

Harvesting deals

Once the takeover/merger has been completed, unforeseen post-deal issues may arise, such as location of control, staff cooperation, duplicate flows of operations, overlapping activities and doubling up of research. The financial advisers will analyze these issues and ascribe priorities to them in terms of ensuring a smooth transition with the end result of maximizing value.

PricewaterhouseCooper operates with the concept of accelerated transition which in a short period of time following the deal identifies and focuses on the 20 per cent of activities in a business which taken together represent some 80 per cent of the deal value in terms of returns from the new entity.

To ensure maximum return, an awareness of post-deal risks is also needed, and the financial adviser will assist in identifying such areas of risk, e.g., in the integration of financial, operational and technical systems.

OVERSEAS TARGETS

Finance advice regarding overseas targets has a wider domain. For comparison purposes, targets' accounts have to be converted from domestic accounting standards to those of the acquirer's home state. A US acquirer would need the target's accounts to be converted into US-GAAP. Companies may also need to be advised on cross-border capital raising possibilities.

For the acquisition of targets overseas, financial advisers with international contacts are to be preferred to local advisers, as they will be able to draw on knowledge regarding the target's local markets, as well as general economic and political conditions, such as the repatriation of dividends and capital.

MANAGEMENT BUY-OUTS/BUY-INS

A management buy-out (MBO) occurs when a business is sold to its own managers. When a team from outside takes over a business, the term applied is a management buy-in (MBI). With the availability of venture capital for such deals, buy-outs/buy-ins are becoming increasingly popular as a way for employees to become business owners, or to inject new management expertise into an ailing business. Corporate financial advisers such as Grant Thornton specialize in advising teams wishing to do a deal, including negotiating with the vendors through to leaving the new management team in place.

Finance for an MBO/MBI deal may be a combination of debt and equity. Mezzanine finance may be raised, e.g., bank finance involving a small equity participation, and possibly a second charge on the company's assets to secure the loan. Mezzanine finance used to be considered risk capital combining conventional bank loans and equity funding. The banker in return received a higher rate of interest for the loan. It is now becoming more mainstream as a method not only for financing buy-outs and buy-ins, but also as acquisition finance. The role of the financial advisers is to advise employees on the best structuring of finance, and to bid and negotiate on behalf of the employees.

A company may also be taken over by an institution, such as a venture capital company (institutional buy-out, or IBO). A deal of this nature is initiated by the vendor company, and negotiations are directly with the institution. The management although important to the future of the company, is not involved in the negotiations. Venture capital firms are usually looking for an exit after a number of years, e.g., three years.

A recent management buy-out in the corporate finance world involved Singer & Friedlander who sold off their corporate finance division in 2000 to a company formed by former directors and staff, Bridgewell Ltd. Following a private placing which raised £10 million of new equity in 2001, Bridgewell is poised to serve the corporate needs of small and mid-sized companies by providing services of M&As, bid defences, company restructuring, flotations on AIM and the London Stock Exchange, capital raising and public to private deals. In July 2001, advised by Bridgewell (lead adviser: Altium Capital Ltd), Kingfisher Leisure PLC accepted Bridgewell's recommendation to accept an offer from Springboard for £12.7 million.

THE CITY CODE ON TAKEOVERS AND MERGERS

The financial advisers and their clients conduct mergers and acquisitions in accordance with the Takeover Panel's City Code on Takeovers and Mergers. In following the code, they minimize the risk of takeovers becoming delayed through litigation of a tactical nature. The Panel, set up in 1969, is concerned with matters of public interest, and works through the Office of Fair Trading and the Competition Commission, previously the Monopolies and Mergers Commission. In the wider European context, the powerful European Commissioner for Competition Policy, Mario Monti, is keeping a watchful eye on mergers that adversely affect competition in national markets, with due regard to the need for companies to be allowed to grow to a size that will enable them to compete on a global scale.

The takeover panel administers the city code and is concerned with takeovers of companies with shares held by the public. Fairness to shareholder is a guiding principle, and this can only be achieved through maintaining fair and orderly markets.

The panel consists of financial and business institutions, with the chairman and two deputy chairmen and three independent members appointed by the Governor of the Bank of England. The present chairman Peter Scott, is a QC, and two deputy chairmen are John L. Walker-Haworth, former managing director, UBS, Warburg, and Antony R. Beevor, senior adviser, SG Hambros.

The panel has been active in making suggestions for the implementation of the EU Takeover directive which has been under preparation for 12 years. It was finally defeated in the European Parliament, failing to gain a majority in a tied vote in 2001.

The panel, in association with the DTI, had worked hard to make the proposed directive acceptable from a UK point of view. Since the directive was a minimum standards directive, it would not have achieved a uniform set of takeover rules in the EU.

M&A ACTIVITY IN 2001

Table 7.1 sets out some of the M&A activity in the UK in 2001 in order of size of deal.

Table 7.1 M&A activity in the UK in 2001 in order of size of deal

Acquired company	Acquirer	Lead adviser	Date in 2001[1]	Terms	Consideration (£m)[2]
Britax International PLC	Seton House Acquisition Ltd	Pricewaterhouse Coopers	09.08.	Recommended cash offer of 147p per Britax share[3]	441
DBS Management Plc	Misys PLC	Dresdner Kleinwort Wasserstein	03.08.	Recommended cash offer of 150p per DBS share with a loan note alternative[2]	75.0
Interactive International Investor PLC	AMP Ltd	Ernst & Young LLP	10.08.	Recommended cash offer of 30p per Interactive Investor share (with a possible further payment)[2]	52.1
Kingfisher Leisure PLC	Springwood PLC	Altium Capital Ltd	09.08.	Recommended cash offer of 90p per Kingfisher Leisure share[2]	12.7

Continued ...

Table 7.1 continued

Acquired company	Acquirer	Lead adviser	Date in 2001[3]	Terms	Consideration (£m)[1]
Cakebread Robey PLC	Jewson Ltd	BNP Paribas	30.07.	Recommended cash offer of 62p per Cakebread share[2]	07.44

1. Declared unconditional
2. Based on the mid-market price on the last practicable date before posting
3. Cash alternative figures are quoted per share

Source: Modified from Hemscott International tables (2001)

THE BIG M&A PLAYERS

Internationally, Goldman Sachs was the top financial adviser for M&As in terms of deal value during the first six months of 2001, with Merrill Lynch & Co., Morgan Stanley and Credit Suisse First Boston in second, third and fourth place. Goldman Sachs' biggest deal was on behalf of American International Group, on their proposed US$ 424.6 billion takeover of American General Corp. The Thomson Financial league table for the US announced mergers and acquisitions by financial advisers based on rank value, shows the ranking (*see* Table 7.2).

CONCLUSION

The financial advisers come into their own when acting in M&A deals. If required, they can identify targets on behalf of their clients, if need be on a confidential basis, and they can establish to what extent and in which areas the proposed target will add value to their client's business. Once a target has been identified, they will act as lead advisers, and negotiate on behalf of their client to secure the best deal. As part of the process, they will oversee a thorough due diligence process. During the negotiations, they will ensure that the proposed deal does not fall foul of any regulatory or voluntary takeover codes. After the deal has been completed they will analyze post-deal issues and recommend ways of ensuring a smooth consolidation.

Table 7.2 Thomson Financial tables for US announced mergers and acquisitions by financial advisers for the first half of 2001 compared with the first half of 2000 based on rank value

| Adviser | First half 2001 | | | | First half 2000 | | Percentage |
	Rank value US$ million	Rank	Market share	Number of deals	Rank value US$ million	Rank	change in rank value
Goldman Sachs & Co	138 370.1	1	36.4	79	395 595.5	1	−65.02
Morgan Stanley	117 717.0	2	31.0	64	383 789.1	2	−69.33
Credit Suisse First Boston	105 221.6	3	27.7	115	235 157.5	5	−55.25
Merrill Lynch & Co. Inc.	77 201.3	4	20.3	49	322 501.6	3	−76.06
JP Morgan	58 827.6	5	15.5	76	121 456.9	7	−51.57
Citigroup/Salomon Smith Barney	50 362.2	6	13.3	73	294 029.2	4	−82.87
Lehman Brothers	29 053.2	7	7.6	47	83 710.7	9	−65.29
Dresdner Kleinwort Wasserstein	20 728.2	8	5.5	13	224 340.5	6	−90.76
UBS Warburg	19 199.4	9	5.1	28	84 251.3	8	−77.21
Bear Stearns & Co. Inc.	15 273.2	10	4.0	43	33 596.3	11	−54.54
Greenhill & Co, LLC	14 894.2	11	3.9	8	1 682.5	31	785.24
Deutsche Bank AG	13 051.4	12	3.4	32	31 061.2	13	−57.98
Banc of America Securities LLC	10 613.7	13	2.8	26	32 854.6	12	−67.69
Lazard	6 724.7	14	1.8	16	35 034.9	10	−80.81
US Bancorp	5 268.2	15	1.4	25	2 422.8	28	117.44
Touchstone Securities Ltd	4 929.2	16	1.3	1	–	–	–
Keefe Bruyette & Woods Inc.	4 322.0	17	1.1	17	2 008.9	29	115.14
Petrie Parkman & Co. Inc.	4 209.8	18	1.1	5	1 575.7	34	167.17
Daniels & Associates Inc.	4 132.6	19	1.1	20	1 565.5	35	163.98
RBC Dominion Securities	4 122.8	20	1.1	10	1 061.8	38	288.28
ABN/AMRO	3 799.4	21	1.0	14	124.5	81	2951.73
FleetBoston Financial Corp	3 659.0	22	1.0	24	17 670.7	17	−79.29
Societe Generale	3 071.1	23	.8	14	8 139.3	20	−62.27
Rothschild	2 635.6	24	.7	7	5 766.9	26	−54.30
CIBC World Markets	2 483.9	25	.7	23	7 065.1	23	−64.84
Deals with adviser	337 996.4	–	88.9	829	831 122.2	–	−59.33
Deals without adviser	42 082.4	–	11.1	3223	55 823.4	–	−24.62
Industry totals	**380 078.8**	**–**	**100.0**	**4052**	**886 945.5**	**–**	**−57.15**

Source: Thomson Financial (973) 622-3100 07/03/2001

Regulatory issues

OVERVIEW

The role of the UK supervisory bodies, the Treasury, the Bank of England and the newly constituted Financial Services Authority (FSA) has been instrumental in providing a framework of financial stability within which the financial advisers and the financial services industry as a whole can operate. The UK financial services sector is more international than any other, and is backed up by the supervisory authorities' commitment to providing a level playing field to all participants, including international newcomers. This combined with openness to technological change, a critical mass of human resources, and an ample supply of supporting services in the field of finance has enabled the City of London to remain one of the world's leading international financial centres.

THE BANK OF ENGLAND

The Bank of England remains responsible for the stability of the financial system in the UK through monetary policy functions and through maintaining the financial system infrastructure, as the bankers' bank. The Financial Services Authority is in charge of financial regulation. However, there is close co-operation between the two bodies. The Deputy Governor responsible for financial stability has a seat on the Financial Services Authority Board. Once all statutory instruments are in place, the FSA will be fully responsible for the supervision of banks, building societies, investment firms, insurance companies and friendly societies; the Financial Services Authority will also 'advise on the regulatory implications for firms, markets and clearing systems of developments in domestic and international markets and of initiatives, both domestic and international, such as EC directives'.

THE FINANCIAL SERVICES AUTHORITY (FSA)

The FSA is the previous Securities and Investments Board (until October 1997), and is a non-governmental independent body with statutory powers to regulate the financial services industry in the UK. Its Board is appointed by the Chancellor of the Exchequer.

The complete transfer of authorized firms and individuals to the new FSA regime was in place by 1 December 2001, under the so-called grandfathering provisions. These provisions were set up to smooth the transition from the old regime, and allowed firms to continue to operate as before following the implementation of the new Financial Services and Markets Act, without having to re-apply to the new authority for permission or approval. Regulated products, such as unit trusts, also benefited from the provisions. A strict timetable was issued by the FSA for the transition to the new regime.

The FSA sets out its four main objectives under the Financial Services and Markets Act as being:

- to maintain confidence in the UK financial system;
- to promote public understanding of the financial system;
- to secure an appropriate degree of protection for consumers;
- to contribute to reducing financial crime.

In pursuit of its objectives, the FSA takes cognizance of the responsibilities of regulated firms' own management, and strives to balance the restrictions placed on firms with the benefits of regulation to consumers and the industry. The FSA is also keen to facilitate innovation in the financial sector, and it recognizes the importance of viewing its responsibilities from an international perspective, through serving the marketplace in a way which enhances the UK's competitive position in the financial services sector *vis-à-vis* the rest of the world.

Single regulatory body

When the Act is fully implemented, the FSA will be the single statutory body for financial services in the UK. The FSA has already taken over responsibility for banking supervision from the Bank of England, and for a number of Treasury functions. The responsibility for listing on the London Stock Exchange was assumed from the LSE on 1 May 2000, and all listing documentation now has to be approved by the FSA before listing can proceed.

In addition, the regulatory functions of the following are being incorporated into the FSA's domain of responsibilities:

- Building Societies Commission (BSC): building societies
- Friendly Societies Commission (FSC): friendly societies
- Investment Management Regulatory Organization (IMRO): investment management
- Personal Investment Authority (PIA): retail investment business
- Registry of Friendly Societies (RFS): credit unions' supervision
- Securities and Futures Authority (SFA): securities and derivatives business.

This has implications for financial advisers, since the FSA's future responsibilities will be to regulate and authorize all financial businesses, as well as unit trusts, and to recognize and supervise investment exchanges and clearing houses.

The FSA's response to 11 September

Following the terrorist attacks on 11 September 2001, the FSA took the lead in responding to President Bush's call for the blocking of accounts of terrorist organizations and individuals by publishing on its website the organizations suspected of money laundering, and by admonishing its authorized firms to check their records for any of the firms on the list and to report all suspicious transactions to the National Criminal Intelligence Service in the usual way.

The FSA also looked into reports that the terrorists had profited from the atrocities through prior trading activities in the markets and noted that 'aggregate trading volumes in the UK regulated markets were high, but not unduly so'. One of the sizeable put options traded in London on airline stock turned out to be on behalf of Lufthansa as part of their hedging strategy. However, the FSA continued their investigations, calling for reports from regulated markets on suspicious transactions, and declared that they 'would leave no stone unturned' in their search. Following the attacks, FSA chairman Howard Davies admitted that there had been 'some unattractive examples of aggressive short selling in recent weeks', and promised to act if necessary, consistent with the FSA's new powers over market abuse.

The FSA's guiding principles

The FSA has laid down a set of high-level principles for investment firms to follow, as follows.

- *Integrity.* A firm should observe high standards of integrity and fair dealing.

- *Skill, care and diligence.* A firm should act with due skill, care and diligence.

- *Market practice.* A firm should observe high standards of market conduct. It should also, to the extent endorsed for the purpose of this principle, comply with any code or standard as in force from time to time and as it applies to the firm either according to its terms or by rulings made under it.

- *Information about customers.* A firm should seek from customers it advises or for whom it exercises discretion any information about their circumstances and investment objectives which might reasonably be expected to be relevant in enabling it to fulfil its responsibilities to them.

- *Information for customers.* A firm should take reasonable steps to give a customer it advises, in a comprehensible and timely way, any information needed to enable the customer to make a balanced and informed decision. A firm should similarly be ready to provide a customer with a full and fair account of the fulfilment of its responsibilities to him.

- *Conflicts of interest*. A firm should either avoid any conflict of interest arising or, where conflicts arise, should ensure fair treatment to all its customers by disclosure, internal rules of confidentiality, declining to act, or otherwise. A firm should not unfairly place its interests above those of its customers and, where a properly informed customer would reasonably expect that the firm would place his/her interests above its own, the firm should live up to that expectation.

- *Customer assets*. Where a firm has control of or is otherwise responsible for assets belonging to a customer which it is required to safeguard, it should arrange proper protection for them, by way of segregation and identification of those assets or otherwise, in accordance with the responsibility it has accepted.

- *Financial resources*. A firm should ensure that it maintains adequate financial resources to meet its investment business commitments and to withstand the risks to which its business is subject.

- *Internal organization*. A firm should organize and control its internal affairs in a responsible manner, keeping proper records, and where the firm employs staff or is responsible for the conduct of investment business by others, should have adequate arrangements to ensure that they are suitable, adequately trained and properly supervised and that it has well-defined compliance procedures.

- *Relations with regulators*. A firm should deal with its regulator in an open and co-operative manner and keep the regulator promptly informed of anything concerning the firm which might reasonably be expected to be disclosed.

REGULATION IN THE US

In the US, the Securities and Exchange Commission (SEC) is the all-powerful regulatory body. It was set up in 1934 to enforce the newly passed Securities Act of 1933, and the Securities Exchange Act of 1934. Its main objectives are to ensure market stability and integrity and to protect investors. The SEC upholds the principle of transparency in market transactions, and accordingly requires all public companies to disclose the required information. This enables investors to draw from a pool of knowledge and, on the basis of the information available, to decide for themselves whether or not to invest in the markets.

The SEC oversees key participants in the securities industry, including stock exchanges, investment advisers, broker dealers and mutual funds. Investment advisers managing US$ 25 million or more of clients' funds must generally be registered with the SEC. The emphasis again is on promoting the disclosure of timely, relevant and accurate information, and on enforcement of the securities laws. Enforcement actions are taken against insider trading, accounting fraud, and providing false or misleading information about securities and companies. In requiring companies to disclose information, the SEC requires the filing of special forms, e.g., for the filing of annual reports (10-K) and quarterly reports (10-Q). Special forms are also required to be filled in for companies seeking an IPO.

The SEC lost vital documents from its enforcement office in the WTC in the 11 September terrorist attack.

REGULATION IN THE EUROPEAN UNION

One of the major aims of the single financial market in the EU is to enable any investment firm, bank or insurance company to offer its products and services throughout the EU, either from its home base, or through representative offices, branches and subsidiaries, or electronically.

The EU's single market's aim to create a seamless integrated Europe has transformed the European financial system and has enabled the consolidation of financial services to progress, with much wider scope for cross-border trading and financial institutions merging on a cross-border basis. However, apart from a few spectacular mergers, merging of banking institutions (Allianz, Dresdner, Nordea/Unibank) across borders has been slow.

MAIN EU FINANCIAL SERVICES DIRECTIVES

The EU has issued a number of directives aimed at regulating and harmonizing the financial services industry with respect to the offering of securities. Most of the directives have now been incorporated into national law by member states. The directives include the following.

The investment services directive No. 93/22/EEC (ISD)

This allows investment firms to offer their services in any member state, subject to the granting of a licence called the Single European passport. This passport is granted subject to the necessary authorization. A proposal for amendments to the directive seeks to iron out remaining difficulties, such as the necessity for financial services providers to conform not only to the rules and regulations of the home country, but also those of the host country.

The Commission in Brussels is currently considering adjustments to the ISD, which is the cornerstone of the EU legislative framework for investment firms and regulated markets, and consultative hearings are being held and opinions sought from high-level representatives from the European Parliament regulators and academic commentators. The financial services industry is represented by Dresdner, Kleinwort and Wasserstein.

The capital adequacy directive No. 93/6/EEC

This covers minimum capital requirements of investment firms and institutions needed for them to operate in the EU under a European single licence.

Offering of securities directives

A set of directives relates to the offering of securities.

- **The prospectus directive No. 89/298/EEC** setting out the information to be provided to investors on offering securities to the public, and the requirements for the drawing up, scrutiny and distribution of the prospectus.

    The need for investor protection is safeguarded through the requirements set out in the directive. The disclosure requirements in the prospectus enable investors to make a proper assessment of the investment risks involved.

    The information in the prospectus should include:

    - Those responsible for the prospectus

    - The nature of the offer

    - The period during which the offer is open

    - Restrictions, if any, on the transferability of securities

    - The markets on which the securities will be traded

    - The place at which the securities are offered, if known

    - Methods of payment

    - The name and registered office of the issuer

    - Details of the capital structure of the issue

    - The issuer's principal activities

    - The issuer's financial position

    - The issuer's administration, management and supervision

    - Any new developments affecting the issue.

- **Proposal for a new 'single passport' prospectus**

    The European Commission has put forward proposals for a 'single passport' prospectus which would be admissible in all member states for companies seeking to raise money in more than one EU national market through a public offering or when admitted to trading. The level of regulation proposed would be uniform, but more stringent than existing requirements. The aim of the directive is to reduce costs for public companies raising money through the issue of shares on an EU-wide basis and to simplify compliance.

Opposition to the new proposals

But the new proposals have met with opposition from several quarters. The UK Quoted Companies Alliance (QCA) has raised the alarm and launched a campaign to stop the proposals from going forward in their present form. The proposals are seen as a threat to the more lightly regulated markets, such as AIM, with the possibilities for start-up businesses to raise funds being reduced. The imposition of the new requirements would mean higher costs for companies seeking a flotation or a secondary fund-raising, and would hit smaller companies particularly hard.

The QCA warns that the new directive could also have the unintended consequence of imposing an increased administrative burden on quoted companies as well as threatening the markets for emerging companies. The proposed requirements for an annual registration would add to the bureaucracy of running a company. The QCA is calling for the new single passport prospectus to be made optional, i.e., only to be adopted by those companies who need it. The prospectus would also impose a regulatory regime, which ignores the fact that most companies do not raise capital outside their home country. This would be particularly hard on small companies.

The QCA also points to the danger that the new strict regime would attract listings away from the EU to overseas exchanges.

Additional costs associated with the implementation of the new EU directive have been estimated by the QCA to be in the region of £150 000 a year for every company, which works out at a total annual cost of £1.2 billion for Europe's companies. The annual additional cost for the UK alone would be in the region of £375 million.

The QCA has submitted comments on the proposal to the EU and HM Treasury, and is liaising with other affected bodies, such as the London Stock Exchange, the FSA, the Association of Private Client Investment Managers and Stockbrokers (APCIMS) and the CBI. British MPs are being lobbied about the Alliance's concerns. There are 59 UK chief executives, directors and quotes companies behind the launching of the campaign.

Added to the voices of concern is a letter from the London Stock Exchange warning that the City of London's views should not be ignored.

Other directives relating to the offering of securities are as follows.

- *The interim reports directive No. 82/121/EEC* on information and reports to be published regularly by companies with a stock exchange listing. This directive set out the requirements for the drawing up, scrutiny and distribution of the listing particulars. The aim is to protect investors through greater transparency.

- *The admission to listing directive No. 79/279/EEC* co-ordinating the requirements for the admission of securities to official stock exchange listing, and its companion directive, *the supplementary listings particular directive No. 80/390/EEC,* co-ordinating the requirements for the drawing up, scrutiny and distribution of the listing particulars to be published for the admission of securities to official stock exchange listing, as amended.

Directives dealing with regulatory issues

Regulatory issues are covered by the following.

- *The disclosure of major shareholdings directive No. 88/627/EEC* on the information required to be published on the acquisition or disposal of a major holding in a listed company. The directive requires shareholders in quoted companies to disclose their holdings when certain percentage thresholds are reached.

- *The insider dealing directive No. 89/592/EEC* co-ordinating regulations on insider dealing. This directive aims to protect the market from insider dealing practices arising from inside information. This concept is defined as 'information of a precise nature which has not been made public, relating to one or several issuers of transferable securities or to one or several transferable securities which, if made public, would be likely to have a significant effect on the price of the transferable security or securities in question'. Such knowledge, if acted upon, could benefit certain investors at the expense of others, and the directive is partly aimed at building up confidence in secondary markets.

- *The money-laundering directive No. 91/308/EEC* on the prevention of the use of the financial system for the purpose of money laundering.

  The directive defines money laundering as the laundering of money obtained through 'serious criminal conduct' (e.g., terrorism, drugs, fraud, counterfeiting, forgery, blackmail, extortion, robbery).

  Regulatory measures against money laundering have been tightened up around the world following 11 September, and in the US, new rules have been issued by the Treasury to include securities firms. The new rules prohibit the use of correspondent accounts with offshore 'shell' banks in tax havens. Many of these banks are limited to their incorporation documents and a small representative presence. Such correspondent accounts are often used for money laundering purposes. But the US securities industry maintains that the practice of operating offshore accounts does not normally apply to brokerage firms.

Main electronic financial services directives

The directives dealing with e-commerce and distance selling and transparency issues affect financial services, but are not solely directed at financial firms.

The e-commerce directive

The provision of electronic financial services is covered by a new directive, the e-commerce directive No. 00/31/EC. The directive was passed in June 2000 and covers information society services provided by electronic equipment, both business-to-business and business-to-consumers, including services provided free of charge and interactive on-line shipping. Sectors covered include on-line financial services and on-line professional services (lawyers, accountants, etc.).

The distance selling of the financial services directive

A new directive on distance selling of financial services has also been agreed by the EU Council of Ministers, but is not yet on the statute book. The distance selling of the financial services directive deals with the marketing of financial products, such as credit cards and pension plans, via the internet, phone or fax as well as direct mail.

The directive bans inertia selling to consumers. Under an opt-in rule, companies would also no longer automatically be able to use unsolicited e-mail to market their products.

The transparency directive

This was adopted by the EU in 1998. Although wider in its aim, this directive also has relevance to the financial services. It covers financial services and financial information offered at a distance (i.e., without the parties being simultaneously present) by electronic means (sent and received by electronic equipment). Through harmonization in the fields of technical standards and regulation, the directive aims at increased transparency in the field of information without regard to national frontiers.

Slow national implementation of directives

Although the single market (of some 340 million people) was established on 1 January 1993, based on the free movement of people, goods, capital and services, many national governments still have not implemented existing community law or enforced it properly, and barriers to trade continue to stand.

Implementing the various pieces of legislation of the single market has been a long and laborious process, and a couple of years ago, a financial services action plan was started, proposing specific measures for integration, to be completed by 2005. Among the steps proposed are future accounting strategies (adoption of International Accounting Standards in member states), and a revision of the two prospectus directives.

CONCLUSION

The UK is one of the best regulated markets in the world. The high standards set by the regulatory authorities (together with the stable economy) contribute to the reasons why so many international finance companies and finance houses choose London as a base: 550 international banks and 170 global securities firms have offices in London. The strict regulatory regime is also a strong argument in favour of attracting international companies to listing on the LSE and AIM. The relatively new Financial Services Authority is increasingly making its voice heard, and its activities are instrumental in helping to maintain confidence in the financial system. The European financial services directives, many of which have now been passed into national law in most member countries, have been influenced by UK regulatory legislation through consultation and lobbying.

Case study – Close Brothers

OVERVIEW

The Close Brothers Group was founded in the City of London in 1878 and used to be part of Goldfields, but following a management buy-out in the 1920s, Close Brothers developed into a company of independent corporate financial advisers. It is now the largest independently quoted merchant bank in the UK, and is among the top 200 LSE-listed companies in terms of market capitalization. Major shareholders are large financial investors.

The group consists of four divisions:

- corporate finance
- banking (including asset finance)
- asset management
- market-making (Winterflood).

Close Brothers Corporate Finance offers the following products and services to clients:

- capital raising
- acquisitions
- trade sales and disposals
- corporate restructuring
- debt advice.

PRODUCTS AND SERVICES

Capital raising

Close Brothers assist companies in raising finance for growth, and have participated in many successful capital raisings on the LSE main market and AIM as well as organizing private equity. For unquoted companies and pre-IPO candidates, Close Brothers have a specialist private placement unit, which will identify and access the most appropriate sources of private equity funding.

Initially, a rounded view of finance-raising is presented to the client. At the early stage (private company, pre-IPO) in a company's fund-raising, Close Brothers will be looking at private placement opportunities, and restricted groups of investors are approached. Interested parties may be HNWIs (high net worth individuals with liquid assets of £100 000 to £1 million), and as one of the pioneers in Wealth Management, Close Brothers have a network of HNWIs who are interested in private placement opportunities. Venture capitalists may also be approached, but they have tended to move up the valuation scale, and are mainly interested in bigger deals in the range £2 million to £10 million. If the business is worth between £5 million to £10 million. specialist funds may be approached.

For bigger companies, Close Brothers tend to remain in an advisory role. If a large company wants to go for a rights issue or a placement of shares, Close Brothers will act as the sponsors and will manage the transaction in partnership with one or more brokers who in turn have relationships with the investing institutions. Close Brothers have also acted as underwriters in the past (Logica).

Acquisitions

In the past decade, Close Brothers have handled some 150 M&A deals. With a strong European presence, a high level of negotiating skills and detailed industry knowledge, Close Brothers are well placed to manage the increasing number of cross-border deals.

The M&A work is the main area of activity, with disposal work, such as the sale of non-core subdivisions, playing a major part.

Some Close Brothers Corporate Finance deals in 2000 and 2001 are listed in Table 9.1.

Table 9.1 Close Brothers: results of 1999–2001 (year-end 31 July)

Date	Deal	Deal value £/euro	Name of client
July 2001	Disposal of DCS outsourcing division to Bridgeport Capital	£21 million	DCS
Jan 2001	Private placement	€24 million	Verigen
Dec 2000	Disposal of DB8, smart card business, to Schlumberger	€350 million	Bull
June 2001	Sale to COLT plc	€28 million	Fitec
March 2001	Disposal of Compelsource to Specialist Computer Holdings Plc	£19 million	Compel
Oct 2000	Acquisition of PDV (Germany) and underwritten fund raising	€590 million	Logica
Nov 2000	Acquisition of STS (Canada) and underwritten fund raising	£272 million	NSB
Aug 2000	Sale to Spectrasite Holdings (USA)	Undisclosed	Aerial Group Ltd
July 2000	Sale to Wireless Facilities International (US)	£15 million	Questus
June 2001	Restructuring of senior and convertible subordinated debt	£750 million	Danka
Sep 2000	Acquistion of ICT Electronics (Spain)	€32 million	Telemetrix
Apr 2000	Acquisition of First Telecom Group Plc (UK/Germany)	£520 million	Atlantic

Source: Close Brothers Corporate Finance

Trade sales and disposals

As well as full-scale M&As, Close Brothers also handle disposals/spin-offs. Clients may wish to dispose of parts of their business due to market forces, or the need to rationalize and concentrate on core products. They may also want simply to raise cash, or shed unprofitable product lines. Close Brothers have handled some 170 disposals during the past ten years, with the aim of maximizing the sales value of the deals for their clients.

Corporate restructuring

Following the exclusive alliance with US associates Houlihan Lokey Howard & Zukin, specialists in corporate restructuring, Close Brothers' capabilities in this area have been strengthened with the setting up of a dedicated unit (end of 2000) to provide advice to companies in financial distress. This area of expertise has become one of the company's strongest offerings. The new unit, CRG (Corporate Restructuring Group) was headed up by Richard Grainger (formerly of Hill Samuel) who has since taken over as Chief Executive of Close Brothers Finance Division.

Debt advice

Close Brothers Debt Advisory Group works as a separate entity offering clients independent advice.

GROUP PERFORMANCE

Group operating profits for the year ended 31 July 2001 were £94.2 million, compared with £155 million in 2000, the first decline in profits for 26 years. This was caused by losses in the Group's market making division, Winterflood Securities, due to a sustained bear market in small caps. Corporate finance/banking, and asset management continued their growth, with profits from these activities increasing by 28 per cent over 2000.

Corporate finance contributed some 12 per cent of the Group's operating profits. During the year 61 transactions were completed, with a value of £6.7 billion.

The banking division contributed some 39 per cent to group operating profits. The division's loan book grew from £0.9 billion to £1.2 billion.

In the asset management division, funds under management amounted to £3.1 billion, and offshore operations were expanded. Equity funds, including technology funds, performed well.

Results for the period 1999–2001 (year-end 31 July) are shown in Table 9.2.

Table 9.2 Close Brothers Corporate Finance deals in 2000 and 2001

	1999	2000	2001
		£ million	
Asset management, corporate finance, banking	45.6	59.8	76.8
Market-making	35.7	109.0	27.4
Operating profit	81.3	168.8	104.2
Central costs	(5.0)	(13.7)	(10.0)
Profit before tax, exceptionals and goodwill amortization	76.3	155.1	94.2

Source: Close Brothers Annual Report 2001

Towards the end of 2001, the corporate finance division's chief executive, John Llewellyn-Lloyds was replaced by Richard Granger, a former Hill Samuel employee. Earlier, Brian Winterflood, responsible for the Group's market-making arm, Winterflood Securities, retired on reaching the age of 65.

Close Brothers Corporate Finance aims to dominate the mid-cap company market, with a growth target of some €2.5 billion. The company's main business is still in the UK, but its partners across Europe contribute an increasing share of the business.

In recent years, the nature of Close Brothers Corporate Finance work has changed. The biggest catalyst for change was the purchase of Hill Samuel's corporate finance department in 1996, with about 40 people from Hill Samuel joining the company, increasing the overall size of the corporate finance division to some 50 people. Since then, the division has grown rapidly, but has recently shed some 10 per cent of staff through voluntary redundancy.

INTEGRATED MODEL OF ADVISORY SERVICES

The company operates in a purely advisory role, and does not handle stockbroking or IPOs. But in general, the market has moved against the traditional UK model of having separate brokers, merchant banks and corporate financial advisers, and is instead moving towards a more integrated model.

CSCF Managing Director Brian Condon has been monitoring the development of the integrated model: 'In year 2000, as the big banks came into the IPO market and started handling the sale of shares, the integrated model began to dominate. During the technology bubble, we found that many of the big banks that did not previously look at £100 million companies, started to target them for IPOs. A lot of stockbrokers also went for the advisory role, and started to build their own advisory services teams.'

STEERING CLEAR OF THE IPO DOT.COM BUBBLE

Close Brothers managed to avoid getting caught up in the bursting of the IPO dot.com bubble almost by default, since they did not have any special IPO expertise, and accordingly took a deliberate policy decision not to become involved in this area.

BUSINESS STRATEGY

Close Brothers are working according to a long-term business model focusing on the provision of advisory services over an extended period. Some clients, such as Logica, have been with Close Brothers for more than 20 years.

SECTORAL APPROACH

Over the past three years, there have been significant changes in the way Close Brothers advisory services operate. Close Brothers has followed the American trend of going for a sectoral approach, and there has been an increasing emphasis on generating credibility with clients in specific sectors. The four main sectors of expertise are the following:

- technology
- business services
- leisure and retail
- advanced manufacturing.

In addition, an energy sector has been set up in the Middle East.

Each of the main sectors has its own team specializing in sector-specific issues, as follows.

Technology group

Advice is given to companies in the TMT sector, as well as biotechnology and the life sciences. Close Brothers support client companies throughout their lifecycle, from early stage fund-raising, through introductions to the capital markets, and growth through M&As.

Clients include Logica, Kewill Systems, NSB, Bull SA and Telemetrix.

Business services group

This group covers companies supporting others through their services, such as recruitment, facilities management, consulting, contracting, transport and distribution. This market is fragmented, with a large number of SMEs.

Leisure and retail group

A number of leisure and retail activities are focused on for acquisitions, disposals and capital raising, including:

- health and fitness and active leisure
- entertainment and attractions
- restaurants
- pubs and breweries
- hotels
- travel and tourism
- gaming and betting
- retail.

Clients include My Kinda Town, Pizza Express, Flying Colours, the Tote, Gremlin Group, Kunick, Regent Inns, First Quench, Cannons Group, Allied Leisure, Heals and others.

Advanced manufacturing group

This group focuses on areas of the manufacturing industry with the following characteristics:

- above average growth
- high R&D expenditure
- high level of IT in product development
- significant level of sub-contracting for non-critical elements
- significant investment in final assembly and testing
- above average level of customer service.

Many client companies are electronics-based.

INTERNATIONAL CAPABILITIES

Clients are increasingly demanding access to international services, and Close Brothers have responded by expanding internationally through the setting up of a network of subsidiaries and associates.

COMPETITION

Competition in 2000 came mainly from the big US firms. However, through re-organization, many of them have become somewhat destabilized, with key staff assigned to specific clients being made redundant. This has given a competitive advantage to Close Brothers who pride themselves on their special on-going personal relationship with their clients.

Close Brothers has seen a decline in activity in the M&A market, with transactions taking longer to complete. Investors are currently very reluctant to commit resources, and many deals will reach a certain stage, and then be aborted. With fewer deals, competition for the deals that are coming up has increased.

The company is competing more and more in the international market, and is therefore in competition with the big international accounting firms that are well ensconced in most western European countries. However, Close Brothers are themselves well-represented in Europe.

INTERNATIONAL EXPANSION

Close Brothers is increasingly going after cross-border deals, particularly in Europe. Their leading international position among UK firms has been created through their European subsidiaries, Dome Close Brothers, Freyberg Close Brothers, Close Brothers International, and in the US market, through an alliance with Houlthan Lokey Howard & Zukin. Through their dedicated Close Associates network of advisers, the company's geographical reach has become global.

LOCAL MARKET ORIENTATION

Close Brothers like to maintain the local characteristics of their international associates and do not believe in sending out expatriates from the UK, except on a programme of secondment to broaden international awareness. Each of the subsidiaries and associates has a strong presence in local financial and commercial markets. Freyberg for instance is a German business, deeply rooted in its home market.

STRATEGIC ALLIANCE IN THE US

In 2000, Close Brothers made a move into the US market through their exclusive strategic alliance with US investment bank Houlihan Lokey Howard & Zukin, with the aim of expanding the two entities' joint M&A and corporate finance capabilities on a global scale. Houlihan is headquartered in Los Angeles and has nine offices around the US plus one in Asia. One of the partnership's first transactions was a financial restructuring deal of US$ 290 million, involving the sale of DSI to Pitney Bowes Inc. The new alliance is already paying off. Joint mandates during 2000/2001 exceeded £2.3 billion.

ORGANIZATION STRUCTURE

Close Brothers has a flat management structure with a short chain of command, and only a few layers of management (*see* Figure 9.1). This structure makes for fast efficient decision-taking and a pro-active business approach. The structure is mirrored in the organization of the Group's finance houses and Associates, which report directly to the Group. With this clear-cut structure, Close Brothers Corporate Finance covers Europe, America and the Middle East, and through its network Associates, the entire world.

Fig. 9.1 Close Brothers: organization chart

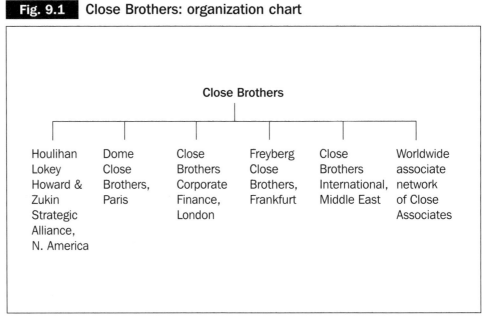

Source: Close Brothers Corporate Finance

DEAL SIZE

Close Brothers' deals typically range up to €1 million for companies valued from €30 million to €2.5 billion. Over the 12 months ended June 2001, the Corporate Finance Division (Close Brothers Corporate Finance Ltd) gave advice to UK and international companies on transactions worth a total of £3 billion and in the second quarter of 2001 alone, CBCF provided advice on deals worth more than £1.8 billion relating to cross-border transactions and international growth strategies. Companies involved included Logica, Telemetrix, Aerial Group Ltd, Go-Ahead Group plc, Bull and others.

FEE STRUCTURE

The bulk of Close Brothers Corporate Finance's income comes from retainer fees and success fees, i.e., fees based on successful transactions. In this respect, their model differs from the US investment banks model. The US banks make a lot of their money from underwriting and the placing of shares with institutions. If a transaction does not go through, Close Brothers do not benefit financially, but they are prepared to share the risks with the fund-raising company to a certain extent. If a public company wants to engage in M& A activity, Close Brothers will be working with a broker. For major businesses, debt advising and corporate taxation advice are provided.

TARGETING THE MID-MARKET

Close Brothers Corporate Finance is active in the middle market and provides independent corporate advisory services to mid-market growth companies with international ambitions. Mid-market companies have developed into a segment in its own right, consisting of high-quality companies with clear aims and strategies, and often with an international orientation. Unlike larger companies who have their own in-house treasury functions and are often looking for more than just advisory services, mid-market companies do not usually employ specialist advisers, and are therefore more likely to seek independent financial advice. Close Brothers see the market as relationship driven and concentrate on personal relationships.

MARKETING

Close Brothers pursue what they call a 're-active marketing programme'. Many clients are won through referrals. Sometimes larger financial advisers will refer smaller deals they do not wish to handle to Close Brothers. Lawyers and accountants are also sources of referrals.

CONCLUSION

Close Brothers is an example of a successful British-based firm of corporate financial advisers, which has grown internationally through gaining a foothold in key strategic locations in Europe and the US and in forming a global network of associates which enables them to serve their clients locally and internationally. Their forward-looking, yet cautious approach in targeting the mid-market has established them as a leader in their field and will stand them in good stead in gaining clients seeking special expertise to assist in overseas consolidation and expansion programmes. However, they have not been isolated from the downward trends in financial markets, and have responded in American fashion by restructuring.

Summary of conclusions

CHAPTER 1

Corporate financial advisers show great diversity on a number of criteria, such as the products and services they have to offer, the way they are operating, the size of their organization, the extent of their expertise, the skill set they have accumulated through practice and experience, and the fees they charge. The selection of corporate financial advisers can be critical for the future success of an organization, and the various factors that combine to make the best choice of corporate financial advisers in any particular case, should therefore be carefully assessed at the highest level.

CHAPTER 2

The top league corporate financial advisers are fiercely proud of earning the prime position in the various ranking tables that are published by commercial organizations such as Hemscott and Thomson Financial. If the advisers are near the top, they will publish it on their website, or incorporate it in their capability statements. The tables also act as a motivational force. The professional advisers at the top of the league will strive to defend their position, and the rest will work harder to move higher. From the clients' point of view, the rankings will provide them with a choice of advisers according to relevant criteria.

CHAPTER 3

Financial advisers in America have developed into high-revenue earners on the back of booming M&A and IPO markets. However, the cycle is currently moving the other way, and the firms are facing tough times ahead. They have had to announce lay-offs amounting to tens of thousands. The financial markets received a devastating blow on 11 September, and are only slowly recovering. The firms are seeking to sustain revenues by broadening the base of the range of products and services they provide, and accordingly, many of the major institutions have become multi-disciplinary centres of financial excellence.

CHAPTER 4

Advising clients on the raising of finance and on the optimal structuring of finance are major weapons in the financial advisers' armoury. The wrong structuring of finance can be a costly mistake. With the myriad of funding alternatives now available in financial markets, specialists are needed to work out the right package of funding for their client. Reputable corporate financial advisers will help their clients avoid pitfalls in choosing ways of raising money. Apart from the more traditional ways of raising finance, the financial advisers will also help their clients consider other ways of raising funds, such as structured finance.

CHAPTER 5

For listings on the stock exchange, the financial advisers come into their own. They will guide their clients through the intricate process of deciding on the best market for the company's shares in terms of liquidity and size, and in terms of the amount of capital the company can be expected to raise. For companies already listed, the financial advisers may assist in preparing for a dual listing. This may be simpler, but there may be hurdles such as differing accounting standards and regulatory regimes. Once a stock exchange has been selected, the financial advisers will assist the company in going forward for listing through a series of steps.

CHAPTER 6

Fund-raising by financial advisers does not normally take place without documentation such as a business plan or a Prospectus, or a private placement memorandum to present to investors. The business plan may be prepared by the company itself, or in consultation with the financial advisers. In the US, business plan consultants may do the work, under the supervision of the company or the financial advisers. A Prospectus underwritten by top financial advisers is likely to get a smooth ride past the listing authorities and to result in successful placement of the issue with the institutions and other investors.

CHAPTER 7

The financial advisers come into their own when handling M&A deals. If required, they can identify targets on behalf of their clients, if need be on a confidential basis, and they can establish to what extent and in which areas the proposed target will add value to their client's business. Once a target has been identified, they will act as lead advisers, and negotiate on behalf of their client to secure the best deal. They will also oversee a thorough due diligence process, and ensure that the proposed deal does not fall foul of any regulatory or voluntary takeover codes. Following deal completion, they will analyze post-deal issues and recommend ways of ensuring a smooth consolidation.

CHAPTER 8

The UK is one of the best regulated markets in the world. The high standards set by the regulatory authorities (together with the stable economy) contribute to the reasons why so many international finance companies and finance houses choose London as a base. The strict regulatory regime is a strong argument in attracting international companies to listing on the LSE and AIM. The relatively new Financial Services Authority is increasingly making its voice heard, and its activities are instrumental in helping to maintain confidence in the financial system.

CHAPTER 9

Close Brothers is a well-established British-based firm of corporate financial advisers, which has grown internationally through gaining a foothold in key strategic locations in Europe and the US and in forming a global network of associates. Their forward-looking, yet cautious approach in targeting the mid-market has established them as a leader in their field and will stand them in good stead in attracting clients seeking financial advice and special expertise for international consolidation and expansion programmes in overseas markets. However, Close Brothers have not been isolated from the downward trends in financial markets, and have responded in American fashion by restructuring.

OVERALL CONCLUSION

■ This Financial Times Prentice Hall Executive Briefing has set out to highlight the role of the corporate financial advisers as accelerators of added value in 21st-century commercial organizations. They also act as creators of wealth for the key players in the organizations they serve. Like their clients, corporate financial advisers are inextricably enmeshed in the unstoppable process of fiscal and commercial globalization.

■ The corporate financial advisers range from niche players specializing in a particular sector or activity (e.g., IT technology, M&A) to fully-fledged financial advisers that have broadened their fields of activity to offer 'one-stop' services on a divisional basis.

■ As part of their ethos, the financial advisers nurture personal relationships with their clients, but this runs counter to the trend in the United States where size and a culture of ever-evolving organizational patterns make personal client contacts more difficult to sustain in the longer term.

- Despite the gloomy economic climate, exacerbated by the events of 11 September, the corporate financial advisers persist in striving to gain competitive advantage and market share for their clients, and they are successfully achieving these aims through their accumulated dedication, expertise and all-embracing knowledge of the workings of financial markets.